WITCH, please

A MEMOIR

FINDING MAGIC IN MODERN TIMES

Misty Bell Stiers

APOLLO
PUBLISHERS

Witch, Please: A Memoir
Finding Magic in Modern Times

Copyright © 2018 by Misty Bell Stiers

Apollo Publishers books may be purchased for educational, business, or sales promotional use. Special editions may be made available upon request. For details, contact Apollo Publishers at info@apollopublishers.com.

Visit our website at www.apollopublishers.

Library of Congress Cataloging-in-Publication Data is available on file.

Cover and interior illustrations and calligraphy by Misty Bell Stiers.
Cover design by Misty Bell Stiers and Rain Saukas.
Interior design by Rain Saukas.

Print ISBN: 978-1-948062-03-9
Ebook ISBN: 978-1-948062-10-7

Printed in the United States of America

For Samaire and Wylie, who remind me every time they smile
we must truly be made of stars;
and Sam, where all the magic in my life originates.

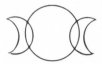

CONTENTS

EVERYONE DESERVES
THE CHANCE TO FLY

INTRODUCTION

W<small>E STOOD THERE ON THE OVERLOOK, STARING OUT AT THE</small> endless stars reflected in the glacial lake below. I had never seen so many. The Milky Way tore across the sky over the miles of forest that surrounded us. The silence enveloping us wasn't silence at all but myriad sighs and whispers that spoke of an abundance of life just out of sight. It truly felt, for that moment, as if nowhere else in the world existed—as if no one else in the world existed. There was only us, and the magnificence of what surrounded us.

It had taken time to get here. I had first met Sam just four years prior, despite the fact that I had grown up around a good deal of his family and he already knew most of my friends. Over the years, these friends had tried to set him up with pretty much every last one of their single friends but me, convinced Sam and I could never possibly get along. (We also lived in different cities for a long time, so I can perhaps forgive them for skipping over me in their matchmaking campaigns.) And truthfully, their assumptions about our possibly incompatible natures weren't too far off the mark. We had a few fiery conversations right at the beginning . . . but they seemed to always drift on into the wee hours once we laid down our verbal weapons and started to really get to know each other. We spent many a night lost in conversation standing next to our cars, stars fading above us as the sun snuck over the horizon.

That said, it wasn't until the wedding of his cousin to a friend of mine that we truly connected. He was an usher and I was the photographer, and an hour before the ceremony we found ourselves being drafted to stand in for the happy couple at the altar so the videographer could set up the shot. It was the first time in almost a decade that I had returned to my childhood church, and I was more than a little on edge. In the years that had passed, I had long since left the soaring ceilings and statues of saints behind for something many might have viewed as an utter failure of my many years of religious education, but had felt to me like coming home. Now here I was in the very place that was supposed to be home, and an overwhelming feeling of not-belonging was haunting me more than a little. As I stood at the altar, awkwardly avoiding eye contact with Sam and any of the aforementioned statues surrounding us, I muttered, "You might want to keep your distance; the odds are good that I'll be struck by lightning any moment." In response, Sam turned me to him, saying, "Well, I suppose we'll get struck down together." What followed were a series of perhaps obnoxiously irreverent vows, given where we were—"I promise to remember your name tomorrow," "I guess we're getting married, then"—that left both of us still smiling long after the videographer sighed and walked away.

He stuck with me, that one. A week after the wedding, I found Sam's smile looking back at me from my computer in what seemed like every shot I'd taken, and I somehow knew he would become more than just a passing acquaintance. We saw each other a few times in the coming months, a truly fun birthday night among friends at Dick Clark's American Bandstand Grill, and dates, just the two of us, to see They Might Be Giants, as well as a night with Béla Fleck and Tim Reynolds, but despite the pull he exerted on my heart, I consciously turned away. I stopped returning phone calls and answering emails. I took the coward's way out for fear if I did anything else I'd change my mind. I had my sights set on an upcoming move from Kansas to New York. Moving to The City had been a lifelong dream, and I wasn't going to gamble on anything that might distract me from getting there. It had meant too much to me for too long. I didn't want to leave a part of me behind. I knew I needed all I had to make it work.

Sam took that decision in stride and, over a year later, when he found himself in New York for work, he gave me a call. The two of us and a dear mutual friend spent the weekend exploring the city, staying up entirely too late, and drinking entirely too much. Days later Sam was back in Chicago, and suddenly New York, the city that trades in teeming sidewalks and sardine-packed subway cars, felt more than a bit empty. I knew then I was really goners. There was no walking away from this man a second time.

So I didn't. Despite distance and time, we figured it all out, and now here we were, feeling like the only people in a vast, amazing world, just four months before we would say our wedding vows for real this time.

Sam had brought me to his family's cabin in Montana to show me what was, in many ways, his true home. My love had lived in what seemed an endless number of towns and cities growing up, moving from refinery to refinery with his dad's job as an engineer with Conoco. But the stories he told most often, the pictures he chose to hang on our walls—somehow, they always circled back around to this place. Here, next to him, there was no mistaking it: this was, if ever there had been such a place, where Sam belonged.

Sam wasn't a believer in organized religion. He had been raised Christian, but held little connection to any church. From the moment I met him, I had known that he was, in every way, his own man—and that included his spiritual practice. He knew what he believed, and he lived it. And he knew from the beginning what I believed, and he supported me in it. He celebrated the changing of the seasons with me, the rise and fall of the light and dark through the year. The connection we had formed over the previous four years was sacred, and his presence in my life was a constant reminder of the magic and marvel that surrounded me.

Now, standing under a velvet sky amid so much of that marvel, I felt like both a tiny speck of existence and a divine goddess.

"This is *my* church," Sam whispered as he wrapped his arms around me.

I took a deep breath of the piney, leafy mountain air, finally feeling at home. I was certain there could be no greater cathedral than this. And I thought, "That will work nicely with what my church is, too."

There's no right way to be a witch—no laws carved in stone, no permanent documents of record. There's no one book to guide you—not even this one. Being a witch simply means learning to own your own power and find your place in the universe. This is the story of how I strive every day to live that truth, and why.

There is wondrous magic in this world; I hope maybe this book helps you find yours.

THAT'S ME
IN THE CORNER

HOW I BECAME WICCAN

IT'S NOT ALWAYS A TORNADO AND A WHOLE HOUSE. SOMETIMES it's just a door.

There is no one way to become Wiccan. In fact, there are as many ways to become a witch as there are witches. That's the beauty of "unorganized religion": you get to pave your own way and find a path that suits you. There are no hard-and-fast rules, no rewards or punishments for good or bad behavior, there is only this exhortation: *Do no harm*. This simple phrase is contained within the Wiccan Rede, a main tenet of our belief system. Essentially, the Rede states that one can live as one chooses, as long as it causes no harm to others. You be you, just don't go interfering with me being me. It's basically our version of the Golden Rule. (Hey, great minds think alike!)

The story of how I landed here, in my witchy ways, isn't too complex. It involved no ceremonial candle burning, no spell casting, and no drawing down the moon. Rather, it's the simple story of how I lost my way and found it again.

It's the story of a closed door.

As I was getting ready to graduate from high school, amidst all the finals-taking and gown-ordering, I was also rehearsing for a final high school theatrical production with some of my very best friends. (Many, to this day, remain some of my very dear friends.) We were staying late at the theater and probably horsing around a bit too much every night. By that point, we had been inseparable for years: acting in every show together, spending weekends on school activity buses, accompanying one another in various combinations to every school dance. The idea that very soon we would not all be together anymore, despite looming over our heads, was still very abstract. In those weeks, it still felt like we would be together, just like that, always—the way things do when you're there, in those moments.

One perfectly ordinary night, parents started coming into the middle of our rehearsal, disrupting the usual flow of things. A couple appeared and quietly took their children out of the theater. Everything started to feel wrong, as if it had all gone sideways. I had a feeling like I might be sick; my chest was tight and I couldn't find my breath. Finally, the director stopped the rehearsal entirely and asked us all to sit down. I remember her asking us to be quiet, and I remember being terrified of the look on her face. She looked . . . broken.

"I have something I need to tell you, and it's not an easy thing. Marc passed away tonight."

I'm sure she said more than that, though I don't remember what. I remember how the words felt, how his name sounded. She cried as she said it. At one point, I think maybe someone else stepped in to tell us more, but if they did, I don't remember what it was. I just remember hearing Marc had died. I know they told us he had committed suicide, but I can't for the life of me recall the words they must have tried to use to soften that blow. I can, however, remember in perfect detail how those words hit my heart.

I was in shock. Marc was the boy who teased me over our backyard fence throughout my entire childhood; the friend who taught me how to use a jigsaw during set construction in the theater while we blasted Garth Brooks on the stereo; the person who gave me my first beer, paired perfectly with a graham cracker and a brilliant laugh. Every year at Christmas, Marc would drive a group of us, packed tightly in his car, up and down the streets of our small town on his very own "Tour de Lights." No matter what we were up to, he always managed to get me home just seconds before my curfew. Marc played a seminal role in my high school experience; we had sung and danced together, built whole worlds together out of plywood and Styrofoam. He had been kind when I needed it most, generous and joyful.

None of that aligned with what people were saying to us in that theater. It just didn't seem possible.

Marc was gone. I couldn't understand how this had happened, how his heart had somehow irrevocably broken without any of us knowing it was even cracked. Despite the closeness we all thought we shared, he had felt alone. Despite our belief that our days together would last forever, he had chosen not to go on. The reality we had taken for granted came to a screeching halt.

The theater seemed unnaturally quiet. Some of the parents who had heard earlier what had happened stood sentinel behind our chairs. People stood and looked around, knowing they should be doing something, anything, but not knowing what was supposed to come next. I desperately wanted to find the friends I was closest to. I wanted to touch them and look them in the eyes and confirm they were here still—that this wasn't the world tearing itself completely apart.

I slowly walked up the aisle of the theater, past the urgent talking and crying that had since erupted after the initial moment of stunned silence. I needed to get out. I needed to get *to*. I don't recall how I got to Marc's house that night to sit in his front yard, or who told my parents where I was going, if they even knew. I remember being one of so very many kids camped there, as if our sheer numbers would bring him back, clinging to the people around us while refusing to believe any of it was real. I don't know what time I went home. I don't know who drove me.

I spent the next days in the company of those friends: piled up like puppies at night in my living room, stumbling from diner to diner listening to bad Muzak versions of Madonna songs while drinking stale cups of coffee and eating giant bowls of canned chocolate pudding, watching movies in someone's basement. Talking of everything but. Talking only of, until our eyes were red and our throats burned. We ignored the rest of the world, desperately holding on to one another, making promises, fervently asking if we were okay. We were scared to death that we *weren't* okay, in ways we couldn't see—the ones that truly mattered now, ones we had never even known existed just days before.

We had realized that we no longer had forever. All we had now was each moment before us, these fragile gifts we weren't entitled to but had been given. It all felt incredibly fleeting and friable, unmistakably not ours to hold anymore.

Eventually, someone insisted we go back to class and finish out the year. We refused stalwartly, until another someone laid down the rule that we couldn't have an opening night for our play without actually having a school day beforehand. So we went home to our separate beds, our separate rooms, to get ready for our first day back at school.

I remember praying we would all make it through the night.

The next morning dawned as if the world hadn't broken. I ate my bowl of Cocoa Krispies, grabbed my backpack, and got in my car. But as I was driving up to the entrance of the school's parking lot, I suddenly just kept going. I couldn't bring myself to walk through those doors just yet. I couldn't face whatever was there—or worse, what wasn't anymore. So I drove to the one place I could think of where I might find peace:

St. Mary's Queen of the Universe.

It wasn't a grand church, but it was mine. I had attended mass there three times a week, plus holy days, from the time I was five until I was twelve, and caught every Sunday after. I knew every nook and cranny of that building. There were—are—thirty-three lights on the ceiling. I knew every shape in the stained-glass windows, every crack in the sculpted wooden Stations of the Cross. It was, in many ways, another home to me.

See, I wasn't just "raised Catholic." My family would never countenance "potluck Catholicism," the term applied to those parishioners who only attended mass at Christmas and Easter and who were perceived as picking and choosing what portions of the doctrine suited them. And I had loved my religion. I attended Catholic grade school, and when that was done, I embraced everything I could outside of mass: I attended Confraternity of Christian Doctrine classes on Wednesdays; I helped clean up the bingo parlor every Sunday night (the smell of sour donuts and burned coffee to this day can bring me straight back to that old gymnasium); I counseled at the church's summer camp; and I was president of our Catholic Youth Organization. I even sat on the state CYO board and helped plan the annual youth conference. I was *Catholic*.

And so, on that morning when everything seemed upside down, when my heart was broken and my soul shaking, I went to the one place I believed could help me find my way through this terrifying maze of reality, or where, at least, I could find comfort. I prayed. I sat in that soaringly empty church and prayed. I cried all the tears that still somehow remained in me and I begged to feel safe again. And when I was all prayed out, I stood and found my way to the rectory. I thought surely someone there could help me.

It was early, the clock just reaching past seven. Morning mass had yet to begin. Even I, in my foggy, mournful teenage state, knew it was too early to knock on that door—on any door, for that matter. But this place—these people—had always had the answers before, and I was desperate for some now. So I knocked.

Father Emil answered the door in the humor you would expect, though honestly, he was never in what one would call a "good" mood. In my experience, Father Emil wasn't at his strongest as a priest of the people—at least not to those of us under the age of crotchety. I admit I was a bit intimidated when he was the one to answer the door; he had been with our parish less than a handful of years, and I didn't know him all that well. In fairness to him, though, he listened patiently as I stood on the stoop pleading my case, asking all the questions he could not answer: the whys and the hows and most especially the what-nexts. It seemed the world insisted on continuing to spin. How was that possible? How could I keep up?

And Father Emil, calmly and quietly, put his hand on my shoulder. "Child," he said, "there is only one thing left to do: pray for his soul. He has committed a mortal sin."

And then he closed the door.

If he had said to me in that moment, "I will pray with you, and God will help you through this sadness," I think my whole life might have been different. I used to wonder: What if he had taken me in to pray? What if he had offered any comfort at all, if he had shown me the compassion I had always associated with my church? When I look back, that moment is such a crossroads, where a small breeze might have been able to blow me back on my familiar course, even if just for a while. Instead, as the door to the rectory clicked into place, something inside me also closed. The world tilted and blurred, and I found myself sitting on the cold cement steps outside, looking with new eyes at what surrounded me.

I envisioned the years I had spent in that place. I remembered the Easter egg hunts on the green, perfectly manicured lawn, in which filling your basket was more a contest in speed than a test of your skill in discovery; the midnight masses on Christmas Eve, when the windows of the church glowed magically in the dark from the candles lit inside; the joy of the acoustic mass, where I sang as loud as I wanted without worrying who could hear my not-so-wonderful voice; the All Saints' Days when, as young children, my fellow students and I dressed up as saints in all manner of sheets, cardboard wings, and giant paper pope hats to parade across the parking lot between cars from the school to the open doors of the church. One by one, my entire lifetime's worth of memories so far wrapped themselves up and moved to a distant part of my heart.

Father Emil was right, of course, according to old-school Catholic doctrine. In that moment, however, I realized that Catholicism was no longer my doctrine. The God I believed in, the God I had thought existed, was merciful and kind. He was meant to love unconditionally. How could I possibly kneel to worship at the feet of a God who would turn away someone whose heart was broken? How could He condemn my friend for breaking under the weight of a world God himself created? I reeled under the sudden realization that the answers I had found at St. Mary's weren't the ones I had sought.

I understood then that if the world would insist on continuing to spin, I would have to make the decision to live as it did so. And if that were the case, I decided, I would need to find a new path to walk along in the indifferently spinning world. This one would no longer work.

I slowly turned away from the building and I left it all behind.

I spent the next few years gradually letting go of many of the things I had once believed. I went through a type of mourning, bidding good-bye to traditions I admit missing to this day. There is something imminently magical about the ritual of Catholicism, the mystery and ceremony of it. Is there anything more transcendent than midnight mass on Christmas Eve? Even after all the years that have passed, I can still close my eyes and feel what it was like in those wee hours of the morning, carols wafting through the great space of the cathedral: the sensation of something surreal happening, the great anticipation of the dawn and all it could—would—bring, the feeling of standing at the precipice of something beautiful and pure.

I longed to find another path whose rituals would speak to me as those moments had, and I tried to come to terms with the fact that while I held dear the moments I'd spent standing in those places, raising my voice in praise, I no longer truly believed in any of it. I began the painful work of sorting through what I believed because it was what I was taught and what I believed because it felt right. It was a messy process.

Part of that process was a sudden and overwhelming feeling of loneliness. I had lived my life up until then accompanied by an omniscient father figure who constantly watched over me, someone who had a plan for my life in its entirety and who never left me. If He happened to be occupied, I had the Holy Ghost or Jesus himself to turn to. And if They were *also* busy with other things, I still had a legion of angels and a host of saints to call on. I was brought up to believe I was never truly alone, and so I hadn't been. In my head and in my heart, I had found comfort in knowing I had my own personal saintly squad. Now, like being unable to clap Tinker Bell back to life, I found that without the faith to power this mighty host, they dropped away. I stood truly alone for the first time.

I wanted to find comfort, to find a place in my world where I would feel less alone, even if that meant having to learn how to be at peace with my own company. I began the difficult process of truly looking inside myself. I needed to know my own heart in order to move forward; I needed to figure out how to live without a legion behind me and to find the power of protection and security I had always sought from those angels and saints within myself. I felt as if I were standing at the bottom of an infinitely tall mountain. Yet slowly, I began my climb, reminding myself that even the great Mississippi River starts, somewhere, as a body of water just steps across. I tried to make at least a temporary peace with my lonely heart.

In doing so, I became annoyingly curious. You know how you're not supposed to talk religion or politics in civilized company? Oh my lord, I was so uncivil. I asked *everyone* what they believed and why. *Tell me!* I couldn't get enough. I borrowed and bought an endless stream of books. I revisited the Bible; I read parts of the Torah and the Koran. I became acquainted with what seemed like endless numbers of Eastern philosophies.

It didn't take me long to realize that the spiritual path I had come from and its closest relatives weren't for me. While I adored the rich myth and allegory of the Abrahamic faiths, their larger organizational structures lost me every time. I had a hard time believing, *really* believing, that there was something outside of myself in charge. And I couldn't come to terms with the notion that there was a select group of people who had more right to call on that something than I did. Beyond that, I just couldn't accept that there was an omnipotent being calling the shots: forgiving with one merciful sweep of the hand, all the while directing a vengeful plague with the other. There was just too much I couldn't reconcile in these ideas, too much I fought against. But oh—the idea of the importance of the mother's line, her connection to her children, in Judaism? *That* sang to me. And did I mention the stories, the amazing tales, that come from all three? I can still listen reverently to the legends of the saints and prophets, the tales of floods and famines and great towers that stretch into the sky.

Alas, it just wasn't me. I eagerly consumed all of the literature, but I couldn't make peace with answering to a singular, unknown being for all the wonder in the world, to being relegated to the status of what felt like a mere pawn in a great game. I didn't want to live a life that would be judged and met with reward or punishment at the end—I had already learned that those doing the judging didn't always play fair. They didn't allow for, well, the *fragility* of humanity. None of it felt true to me, as much as I had hoped it would. Finding peace in any of these places somehow felt like I would be playing it safe, because they were connected to my beginning: they shared the roots, if not the branches. They just weren't mine anymore.

The Eastern philosophies had their own wonderful myths to share, their own cast of great and magical characters with which to fill my imaginings of the world. I adored the complexity and drama of Hindu and Buddhist lore. These tales were so different from the stories I knew, and yet absolutely familiar. They, in turn, led me to rediscover the classical Greek and Roman myths I had read and studied on my own as a child. I loved revisiting the stories my dad had excitedly shared with me when I was small, on afternoons spent envisioning the heroes and heroines, the gods and the Titans. I had always loved trying to imagine who I would be in these stories, who we were most like, who would triumph in the end.

I became entranced with the overlap of themes and creatures that appeared across all of these great myths. I gathered the stories like so many beautiful puzzle pieces: tales from the Egyptians and Greeks, the Romans, the Norse. I made a game of trying to seek parallels among them all—Aztec to Hindu to Christian to Greek. The commonalities seemed never-ending. In the end, I found they were all more similar than I had previously thought possible.

I also realized something else important. These great books, these tenets of faith, I consumed them like literature. I wasn't finding my truth there. I wasn't feeling connected, I was only playing at connecting them. It wasn't the same.

And so, after reading countless books, attending numerous church services and some truly wacky prayer circles (A church of psychics! Who knew such a thing even existed?! The one I found was in Sarasota, Florida, and I highly recommend a visit, for curiosity's sake if nothing else; it was frightening and fascinating all at once), I still had found nothing that felt quite right. What I had discovered was that most religions all believed in basically the same thing: Live a good life. Try not to be an asshole.

I was completely down with that, but I wanted more. I wanted to find a spiritual home. I missed the one I'd previously had; I felt unanchored in a way I had a hard time putting words to.

Then one night in my second year of college, as I sat in my friend Karen's dorm room, she mentioned she had a book she thought I should read. It was yet another book about religion, which she knew was right up my alley. The book was called *Drawing Down the Moon*, by Margot Adler. My heart skipped a beat at the possibility: something new! Then she explained that the friend who had sent it to her was a practicing Wiccan.

What?

Um, no.

I was looking for a spiritual path—I was not looking for a Goth make-over. I immediately put the book down. She insisted I take it, assuring me it was right up my alley—all about that "what-makes-the-world-spin mumbo jumbo." She pointed out that at the very least I would discover what paganism was all about; I might as well round out my research. So out of reluctant curiosity and, truthfully, being too lazy to continue finding reasons not to, I caved and brought the book home with me. In the midst of a fit of insomnia weeks later, I cracked it open.

I read it twice.

I was Wiccan—no incantation or ceremony needed.

In the end, finding a spiritual home wasn't entirely as easy as turning my back on a closed door—it required me to not give up on finding an unlocked window. Eventually I found a path of my own, a line of belief that felt right to me. Wicca was both something I could hold on to and something I could define on my own. It was exactly what I needed. It was *me*.

I know it's not right for everyone. Something I've held on to all these twenty-plus years since leaving Catholicism is the idea of how wonderful this world is, how amazingly fantastic it is that it provides so many paths to peace, so many traditions to walk in, that we can all find something that fits. I don't believe in any one universal truth. I believe we all do our best with what we have and what feels right—that whatever great power spins this world also gives to all of us the capacity to find a way to inhabit wonder. There is the possibility of enlightenment and harmony for all to find, if only we wish to find it.

That's the true magic that exists in this world.

And I should know about magic. I'm a witch.

I can say I'm a witch with confidence now, but it took me years to get here. In theory, becoming Wiccan made perfect sense; the beliefs and system around it spoke to me like nothing else I had previously found. It seemed natural to me to recognize the turning of the year, to call to attention the points of change and pause to recognize them. I felt absolutely at home building traditions around the solstices and equinoxes, recognizing how the darkness of the winter and the brightness of the summer could affect my being, figuring out how to embrace the natural turning of the world and find my place in it. I began to follow the phases of the moon and fell in love with the idea that every month there was a chance to start anew. Always, no matter what else was happening, the cycle of reinvention and reemergence continued. I learned that even the moon took time to disappear and find quiet before it allowed itself to grow as big as it could and shine bright. I started to feel connected to the world around me like I never had before. I began to feel less lonely.

Yet when I went to learn more—wanting to research in order to be sure, to understand, to find answers to the questions that now popped up in my head on a regular basis—it became outrageously intimidating. Suddenly I was right where I had thought I'd end up, where I had feared to be from that first moment when I saw the book in Karen's dorm room. At Pagan Pride festivals and coven meetings, in small occult stores and workshops, I found myself surrounded by people whose names sounded fetched out of fairy tales, images of black candles and smoky cauldrons, books enticing me to cast spells for love and money and luck. At first glance, I found none of the pillars of belief that had so called to me before. Instead, I found every stereotype I had ever heard or imagined. I felt lost in an itinerant Renaissance faire, surrounded by pixies and people who saw witchcraft as more Eastwick than east rising. I started to doubt where I was and whether this spiritual journey was truly right for me. Still, I couldn't shake the sense that this was it. I wasn't willing to give up this place of peace I had found over a few black corsets and spiked jewelry. I thought there had to be more—or rather, less.

It took a few awkward coven meetings and even more awkward conversations before I learned the phrase "solitary practitioner." Someone I had become friends with (the original source of the book I borrowed from Karen, in fact) eventually shared with me that he wasn't so into the whole coven thing and the culture of a lot of it and had found his place as a Wiccan who chose to follow the basic tenets without involving himself with a coven—he simply lived life as a witch, in the way he chose to define that. This seemed revolutionary to me. It changed the way I saw myself as Wiccan—it helped me truly see myself as Wiccan.

With this new perspective, something began to turn in my heart. Step by step, season by season, I became a routine practitioner. I began to talk about it freely, and being a witch started to be just another aspect of who I was. I began to meet other witches like myself, people who practiced as one part of their rich and varied lives. I attended a few more covens, different from those where I'd started; this kind had bread and wine and children sleeping in the background. Yet even when coven meetings were blanketed in normality, I still fell back into practicing alone. It just felt right.

Wicca might be slightly disappointing if you're looking for a grand initiation ceremony on which to hang your proverbial pointed hat. As I said before, there are as many ways to become a witch as there are witches. Don't get too down in the dumps, though—there are a few traditions that are widely accepted. It's up to you to find what fits best. In fact, if you Google "Wiccan initiation" you will find a bombardment of scripts, templates, and guidelines from which to choose. There are different tactics for different situations and different kinds of covens, as well as a number of options for solitary practitioners. These traditions do not vary much in the heart of what they are, but how detailed and involved they are depends on the witches carrying them out. Some ceremonies involve dedicating oneself to a specific god or goddess, some include a sort of personal introduction to the god and goddess, some are simply a welcome into the existing community. Most involve a core ritual of clearing a space, stating your intention, and declaring your willingness to continue a lifelong journey following the Wiccan creeds.

I had no ceremony that made it official. I hadn't necessarily ever thought of creating such a moment; I didn't start this journey with the intention of "ending" somewhere. However, as I became more and more comfortable with what I believed and how that belief was labeled, I became more comfortable with saying out loud that I was Wiccan. At that time and place in my life, those words didn't always bring the warm and welcoming response I would have liked. More often than not, I was treated as if it were a passing phase or a trend I was following—not the true spiritual path I felt like I was on. At times, I let this shake me a bit, let it seep into those most vulnerable places in me and tell me that where I was finding my footing wasn't really solid ground. Every time I felt my foundation shift a bit, I would be at once disappointed and angry at myself. I knew in my heart I had found a set of beliefs that felt true; I knew the path I was on was meant for me. I just needed to find the strength not to let the dismissiveness or derision of others make me feel lesser.

In most any other religion, I realized, there would have been a "moment"—a time when I formally decided to join the community, to proclaim my commitment to a set of beliefs. As a solitary practitioner, though, such a public ceremony wasn't in the offing for me. But I thought perhaps the movement and meaning of that kind of ritual wasn't about the outward declaration so much as the inward promise. I had been practicing for a handful of years, and I knew I wanted to continue. But thinking that to myself was different from taking the time to truly process what it meant and honoring that decision in a more formal way. So I began researching rituals of initiation into Wicca. As I mentioned earlier, I found no shortage of resources. I read books and looked through websites, but in the end I threw most of that research away.

In the end, in my quiet little house in the middle of a quiet little street, I just did what felt right.

With the Wiccan pentacle in mind, I carefully created five cairns in my backyard. I set out a small stack of stones for each point, representing the five elements: sky, earth, wind, water, and spirit, the topmost point. I sat down in the middle, the giant Kansas sky soaring above me. I stilled my body and breathed deep. I felt the earth anchor me and the stars pull me skyward. I felt my place.

I quieted my spirit and I honored it. I thanked what surrounded me for including me in the miracle of life, of creation and forward motion—for allowing me a place in the great turn of the wheel. I promised to walk that wheel as best I could, to recognize my place in this greater miracle, and to bring light and well-being to the world as best I could as I traveled my path. I promised the ground that held me and the sky that covered me that I would remember that I, in fact, possessed no special power, no access to ruling abundance. I was part of the turning wheel, a fragment of the greater abundance of nature. I would bring light wherever and whenever I could, as small as it might be; I would draw my strength from the moon and the stars and the sun. I would use the divinity within me to celebrate and honor the divinity that surrounded me. I would do no harm.

There was no one else present, no promises I made out loud. Yet from that moment on, I held in my heart the oath I had sworn to myself. I vowed to live what was true for me, to follow this path wherever it might lead, actively seeking peace and joy along the way.

It was all I needed. I had already lived a life surrounded by the kind of grand ceremonies that inspired awe, ones that took place in even grander settings: rites led by men in ceremonial garb holding up golden treasures and speaking in ancient languages I couldn't understand. I had sat in the homes of gods, the archways soaring above me, their stories spelled out in giant statues surrounded by candles and windows of colored glass that made me feel small. I was ready to own my own power. I was ready to make a promise to myself that I would live in that power instead of seeking it outside of myself.

I would not ever let myself feel small again.

In the years since, I have faltered on that promise a number of times. I have, at times, let circumstances both within and without my control lessen me. I have let people make me feel unimportant and unnecessary.

And yet I come back to that long-ago promise again and again. It holds me up and reminds me of who I can be: I am divine. I am powerful. I am a vital part of an ever-expanding universe whose limits are unknown and indefinable. I am one child in a long line of survivors; my mere presence is their testament. I am made of the memories of trees, of the wind, of the sun as it shone upon generations of women and men who walked before me, leaving footsteps I never saw, but whose challenges and dilemmas, whose victories and triumphs were the foundation of who I was to become.

I am but a speck in a grand image I will never see the totality of, and yet I am a creator. I, too, am leaving footprints. I, too, am clearing the way for those who will come behind. I draw on the mothers who came before me; I reach toward the children ahead. I am not alone. I am not singular. I am worthy of the power of the universe. I am myself, and that is an amazing and fantastic thing to be.

When I falter, I call upon that, on the knowledge that I am a connection. I am part of something great and grand—not because I was placed here, not because I am a dream of someone's fraught night, but simply because I have a place on the wheel of our world. I am intertwined with all before and all ahead of me. When I need strength, I call upon that.

Rarely has that strength served me as well, or been as important, as when I was in the hospital bringing my second child into the world. Up to that point, things had been pretty easy. Both of my pregnancies had made me feel more beautiful and more connected to the greater world around me than ever before. I was participating in the greatest cycle one could; I was growing life inside me. I reveled, amazed, in the fact that the love I shared with Sam had resulted in such a miraculous and extraordinary thing. I loved being pregnant; Sam joked, when our first child was weeks late, that I was refusing to share her with the world. He was not entirely wrong.

Samaire, our oldest, was born quickly, thanks to some encouraging via castor oil and my amazing midwife. I was only in labor for a few hours and only in the hospital for forty-five minutes before I was holding my small babe. The days following her birth were the most exhausting I have ever had, yet I remember moments in which I reminded myself that I was following a path that had been carved out by other women for millennia before. I was acutely aware as I rocked my babe, as I nursed her, as Sam danced her to sleep, that we were living out a story that had been written across the ages. We would survive, and we would thrive, as others were doing all around the world. That feeling was such a powerful thing: we were absolutely not alone.

Wylie's birth was different. My labor with him was long and frightening. He was turned, essentially stuck, his heartbeat erratic. There were what felt like throngs of doctors and nurses in my hospital room, all ready to immediately jump into action once he was out. There was talk of prepping me for a C-section, then talk of it being too late. I was horrified and scared. I had torn a ligament in my rib cage and every push was torture, yet every push also felt inadequate. All I wanted was respite.

I knew something was wrong, and I was more frightened than I had ever been, but my midwife, Sandy, an older woman who I am convinced was some sort of shaman in a former life, leaned close to my face in the midst of the chaos.

"Misty!"

I tried desperately to focus on her. I made her my world.

"Where is this fear coming from? You are strong, and you will birth this baby when I tell you to. You can do this. You *will* do this. You are his mother. Bring him here!"

I made her voice my lifeline and I closed my eyes. I let myself fall into a black hole where there was just a singular act of intention. I drew from the deepest place in my heart, the place that was still feral and fierce—the place where my natural instincts overruled my fear—and I pushed.

I didn't quite realize, at the time, how serious it was. All I knew was Sandy had told me I needed to get it done, and I could hear fierceness in Sam's voice when he told me I had to do this for Wylie. The whole room seemed to crackle with energy as the nurses and doctors, waiting anxiously to get to work, cheered me on.

I heard very little of it aside from Sam and Sandy's voices—Sandy telling me when or when not to push, Sam reminding me who I was working for. It seemed to go on forever, and with every breath I tried to fill my lungs with the strength of every mother who came before me, every goddess ever created. I would not fail. My body was absolutely weak at this point, but I was determined my spirit would remain strong.

There was a last, monumental push, and Sandy yelled, "Stop!" The room fell anxiously silent, and I waited for the sound of my son's voice.

I didn't get to hear it. The umbilical cord was wrapped around his neck; he was essentially trapped in a noose. Sandy expertly untangled him, and the nurses and the emergency room pediatrician surrounded him and Sandy. Still there was no cry, no breath. My heart stopped. I repeatedly asked if he was okay, and no one would answer me. I asked over and over, getting louder each time, but all I got in return was silence. My heart actually broke later when I asked Sam why he didn't answer me and he replied, "Because I didn't know, and I didn't want to lie to you."

Eventually Sandy grabbed Wylie by the ankle and turned him upside down, and as he hung there she smacked him harder than I ever would have thought possible from someone whose job it was to work with newborn babies. Again, she smacked him. Then she turned him over and sucked fluid out of his mouth, and I heard the sweetest sound possible: my baby cried.

I rejoiced, as have countless mothers before, grateful to have avoided the heartache some have had to endure. We had survived, all of us. Our story continued on, joining the legacy of stories that had come before.

It's easy to look at the births of my children and see a point where our lives were forever altered: the moment I finally had them in my arms, when Sam finally got to feel their realness, to know them as I had for months. But change doesn't always—perhaps not even usually—happen like that. More often than not, change creeps in slowly, washing away the past bit by bit until you look around and realize you have come to a new place.

As it turned out, Father Emil closing that rectory door was a beginning, not an end. My journey from there to here, all the time in between, *that's* when I became a witch. I'm still becoming one, in fact. I may never be done with this journey and I am glad for that. There is always more to learn, more to practice, ways to be better.

I am a witch because I choose to make it so. I make the choice every day because it helps me be my most authentic self. I can point to that door all those years ago and see a beginning, but all the moments that followed are an undeniable continuation of that story; they have added up to where and who I am today. At times, I have stumbled. I have felt lost. I have felt alone and powerless. But I have always found my way back, because I am irrevocably tied to a vast and ever-expanding universe. Like that universe, I am inexplicable and indefinable and ever changing. I have the power of that first initial spark of creation inside of me, at my disposal.

So do you.

In my heart, I know this is true.

A LITTLE FAITH AND
A LOT OF HEART

I AM PROBABLY, ON THE WHOLE, A FAIRLY DISAPPOINTING WITCH. I'm sorry not to have admitted this up front (here you are, so many pages in!), but it is absolutely true. My wardrobe is light on black robes and crushed velvet, and I've never quite mastered the application of a nice thick eyeliner. I don't go in much for magic candles or power crystals, and the closest thing I have to a reliable, repeatable spell is a really delicious banana bread recipe. I keep a broom and use it in my practice, but not to fly, and I follow the phases of the moon, but for watching when it's good to begin new things, not so much for frolicking beneath.

As with many things, the myth of the witch is often more intriguing than the reality. I am a normal mom and wife. I have a job I go to every day in a normal office building. I have friends and family I don't get to talk to enough. I lose track of my keys at least three times a week, and on more than one occasion I have become distracted by this or that and burned whatever I had going on the stove. In no way could I be described as mysterious or otherworldly. I hold no special presence. I can't even read your tea leaves.

I am a red-and-purple-haired fortysomething trying to enjoy life and find her way. I am just like everyone else.

Also, I'm a witch.

That last thing seems to set me apart a bit, which I'm more than okay with—except for the fact that I think, truly, there's a bit of witch in all of us. Who among us hasn't reveled in the sight of an endless, starry sky and felt absolutely astonished at whatever small part in that great mystery we must play? Who hasn't found themselves falling into a series of unexpected synchronicities that lead us just where we need to be when we need to be there? Who among us hasn't found themselves in a place where, even if only for a moment, it feels as if we have succeeded in manifesting our innermost intentions? Embracing life as a witch is often not at all what people think, nor what they expect.

You'll rarely see me traveling to great meet-ups full of pagan revelers, and I don't agonize over incantations to bring my family or myself more luck or love or money. That's just not what Wicca's about—not to me. Even the fact that I call myself a witch is a bit off, as great swaths of Wiccans prefer to avoid that label because of all the connotations it carries. Not surprisingly, most Wiccans would rather not be associated with green skin, magic wands, and nefarious concoctions. (All those poor newts, stumbling around without eyes!) Witchcraft in general, actually, is not synonymous with Wicca. Wicca is a religion based on old witchcraft traditions. Witchcraft itself is not a religion, but rather the acts taken to practice. It is a *craft*, not a belief system. So, in fact, it is possible to see oneself as a witch and not be Wiccan, just as I can see myself as Wiccan *and* a witch. (I have found over the years that calling myself a witch works as a great introductory shorthand to explain what I believe, if not exactly how I practice.) It is also possible to be pagan and not Wiccan, just as someone can be Christian and not Catholic.

Wicca, at its heart, is a relatively new spiritual practice that is often misrepresented to the general public. Wicca isn't spell casting or tarot card reading, nor is it necessarily the female-empowering and goddess-centered religion some believe it to be, though all of the above could very well be part of someone's personal practice. First and foremost, Wiccans (or "witches," if you are talking to someone like me) understand the power of intention— the power of prayers, worship, and rituals to affect their environment and help provide guidance in solving the challenges that enclose them. They seek to live in greater connection to the world around them, in order to better draw and harness its energy and their own to affect circumstances.

Perhaps disappointingly, Wicca is not even associated with those famous "witches" of Salem, or with any number of men and women who fell victim to the mob mentality of witch hunts—people who suffered greatly under the ignorance and fear of their community. Very few of those victims, if any, were witches in any true religious sense. More than likely, a great majority of the people who suffered as a result of witch hunts anywhere were simply men and women who lived on the outskirts of society, who failed to fit in and behave in very specific and accordant ways. The overly independent woman was often seen as a threat, someone who could certainly be in league with the devil. Midwives and healers were also common victims, as they could be easily blamed for sickness and disease when their skill or knowledge wasn't enough to help those who sought their assistance.

So while history is full of witches, none of them were Wiccan—not officially, at least. Wicca, in the grand scheme of history, is still shiny and new. It has its roots at the turn of the twentieth century, when it first began as a spiritual practice, and it only began to gain noticeable traction in the 1950s. There are books and websites galore that chronicle who said what and when first, but the simple truth of the matter is that while some of its practices, rites, and traditions are centuries old, Wicca itself is rather new—and definitely growing. The City University of New York's 2001 American Religious Identification Survey found that Wicca was the country's fastest-growing religion, with 134,000 adherents, compared with 8,000 in 1990. Later, in an updated survey by two of the same researchers in 2008, those numbers had more than doubled from 134,000 to 342,000. Religioustolerance.org estimated the number had increased to 2 million adult Wiccans by the end of 2015. Each year it grows even more.

In fact, Wicca as it exists specifically in North America isn't much older than I am. It was only in 1973, one year before I was born, that seventy-plus practitioners gathered to form the Council of American Witches. Together, they created a document to define exactly what Wicca encompassed. The document was meant to serve a few purposes: it was meant to clarify and define the many different beliefs being practiced under the term "Wicca"; counter the growing amount of misinformation regarding the practice; and officially legitimize the religion, helping it gain governmental recognition. (In 2007, the Wiccan pentacle was recognized as an approved emblem for gravestones by the Veterans Association, allowing deceased Wiccan veterans to rest in peace beneath a symbol of their faith.)

I can't imagine how difficult that task must have been, and yet the council came up with thirteen (of course) pillars, the "Principles of Belief," that are at once inclusive and guiding without being directorial or prescriptive, defining points that remain purposefully vague. They did not define a single practice but rather made an effort to encompass the many belief systems found under the heading of Wicca. The council was so sensitive to the need for the Principles of Belief to be inclusive and leave adherents with free rein that after accomplishing its purpose, it disbanded in 1974, so as to leave no official hierarchy intact.

HERE IS WHAT THEY LEFT BEHIND:

1. We practice rites to attune ourselves with the natural rhythm of life forces marked by the phases of the moon and the seasonal quarters and cross-quarters.

2. We recognize that our intelligence gives us a unique responsibility toward our environment. We seek to live in harmony with Nature, in ecological balance, offering fulfillment to life and consciousness within an evolutionary concept.

3. We acknowledge a depth of power far greater than that apparent to the average person. Because it is far greater than ordinary, it is sometimes called "supernatural," but we see it as lying within that which is naturally potential to all.

4. We conceive of the Creative Power in the universe as manifesting through polarity—as masculine and feminine—and that this same Creative Power lies in all people, and functions through the interaction of the masculine and feminine. We value neither above the other, knowing each to be supportive of the other. We value sex as pleasure, as the symbol and embodiment of life, and as one of the sources of energies used in magickal practice and religious worship.

5. We recognize both outer and inner, or psychological, worlds— sometimes known as the Spiritual World, the Collective Unconscious, Inner Planes, etc.—and we see in the interaction of these two dimensions the basis for paranormal phenomena and magickal exercises. We neglect neither dimension for the other, seeing both as necessary for our fulfillment.

6. We do not recognize any authoritarian hierarchy but do honor those who teach, respect those who share their greater knowledge and wisdom, and acknowledge those who have courageously given of themselves in leadership.

7. We see religion, magick, and wisdom in living as being united in the way one views the world and lives within it—a world view and philosophy of life which we identify as Witchcraft, the Wiccan Way.

8. Calling oneself "Witch" does not make one a Witch—but neither does heredity itself, nor the collecting of titles, degrees, and initiations. A Witch seeks to control the forces within her/himself that make life possible in order to live wisely and well without harm to others and in harmony with Nature.

9. We believe in the affirmation and fulfillment of life in a continuation of evolution and development of consciousness that gives meaning to the Universe we know and our personal role within it.

10. Our only animosity toward Christianity, or toward any other religion or philosophy of life, is to the extent that its institutions have claimed to be "the only way" and have sought to deny freedom to others and to suppress other ways of religious practice and belief.

11. As American Witches, we are not threatened by debates on the history of the Craft, the origins of various terms, or the origins of various aspects of different traditions. We are concerned with our present and our future.

12. We do not accept the concept of absolute evil, nor do we worship any entity known as "Satan" or "the Devil," as defined by Christian tradition. We do not seek power through the suffering of others, nor do we accept that personal benefit can be derived only by denial to another.

13. We believe that we should seek within Nature that which is contributory to our health and well-being.

As you can see, the guidelines themselves are nothing new: honor the earth and your place in it, recognize the divine in every living thing, do no harm. They nod to the acceptance that there is a greater power in the world than most people recognize, but add the potential for us all to harness that power in ourselves for good. They do not acknowledge the existence of Satan or of demons; Wiccans do not worship or believe in the devil. They declare that there is a balance to everything, and what contains darkness also contains light. Neither is good or evil; there is a place for both. Wiccans celebrate that balance; we recognize the need for it. For those who practice

Wicca, true wisdom is living in harmony with the universe. That is where our magic lies.

Being a witch is a truly personal choice. It's no more or less than deciding to hold certain beliefs and live them as best you can—in that way, it's like any other religion. What is different about Wicca is the *personal* part of the choice. There are no strict rules or clear definitions. Each practitioner decides whether to be part of a group (join a coven) or practice alone (become a solitary practitioner, like me). The details of how to practice, what that means and entails, are entirely up to the individual witch.

In fact, I think that independence was possibly the hardest thing for me when I first started practicing. I had grown up under a religious system that had an answer for everything: Where do we go when we die? Why? What should I do if I do something wrong? How do I get something I want? Where did I come from? What specific rules should I live by? What is right? What is wrong? The Catholic Church had answers to all of these questions. There was very little personal choice involved, aside from whether or not to follow the rules. So I followed them, as best I could. And when I put those rules away, I admittedly felt a little lost. Yet, through some honest soul searching, by moving forward one step, one situation at a time, I have slowly discovered I don't need rules. If I know what I believe and what's true to my heart, I already know how to live my life.

When I first read through the guidelines the Council of American Witches put down, they spoke to me because they intuitively made sense. They connected with me in a way no other such document, or book, ever had. They still do. These were rules I could get behind—the kind that really weren't rules at all.

PUNISHMENT AND REWARD

Choosing Wicca as my path didn't just hand me answers. In many ways, it had me searching for them all over again. I was asking myself some big questions, and I wasn't always able to immediately find a response. In fact, I'm still asking myself big questions. And of course, all those years ago, thinking about the events that had led me out of my former faith and onto the path toward a new spiritual practice, I started with one of the biggest ones: What happens when we die?

Figuring out how I felt about this question, the answer to it that I already felt I had, allowed me to live and breathe a belief that had remained hidden in my heart since long before I left the Catholic Church. It never quite sat well with me, the notion that after our spirits left our bodies, they were supposed to arrive before a jury of our peers or an omniscient, godly judge to have our merits weighed and counted. I never understood how anyone's singular life could be fairly punished or rewarded. (This is the point in the discussion where my husband inevitably reminds me of Hitler and a handful of other horrible historical figures, and yes, I get it—but aside from the very obvious, how many people's lives can really be weighed in such a way?) And after that judgment, then what? What is heaven? Hell? How could an all-merciful god who created every human possibly consign some of his own creations to eternal damnation?

I just didn't get it. When I was small, it terrified me—which is, of course, the whole point. As I got older, I became less terrified and a lot more obstinate. The rules of heaven seemed ever changing: Do you have to accept Jesus as your savior? What about all the people who don't believe in Jesus but are living what they believe to be good lives? Are there exceptions? How does it work? How do we know? What about purgatory, the great waiting room, from which if I just pray hard enough I can release my family and friends into the greater good—how does that work? Why can't I pray someone out of hell?

Now, don't get me wrong—all of these questions are answerable, at least if you have faith in the system. But I always struggled with those answers, and I now understand why:

I never truly believed in the system.

In the process of researching other belief systems, of course, I had encountered many different beliefs about death. I went back again and studied the Abrahamic viewpoints and found that they simply didn't speak to my heart; I was intrigued by the Islamic idea that death was just a gateway to another world but got lost once I got to the details.

Old legends enthralled me: Valhalla and Folkvangr seemed filled with such honor, though I have never been much of a warrior, at least not the kind I think they were looking for. I was fascinated by the views of the Egyptians, the idea that the degree to which you were alive or dead was tied directly to the relationships you nourished with those around you. You could be physically alive, but if you were withdrawn from others you were viewed as being much closer to dead than someone who might be physically dead but fondly and actively remembered. That notion spoke to me in ways of which other philosophies had fallen short. But again, I was lost in the details.

I adore the idea of reincarnation. I'm a sucker for a second chance—or a third. Or an eighth. I want to believe that I will meet my husband and love him wholeheartedly through every coming lifetime, and if I'm given that chance, I know I will. I will seek him out with everything I have.

But in my heart, I'm just not counting on it. My truth is different: I believe this may really be it. This world, as flawed and hurtful and cruel as it can be, may be as good as it gets. (I realize that sitting on this pile of privilege allotted me by place and time and other circumstances of birth makes that idea perhaps easier to swallow for me than it might be for those who don't share my good fortune, but all the same, it's my truth.) When we die, I now believe, our tale simply ends. There are no more first loves, no more first steps, no more grand adventures. It doesn't mean we end, of course. Our spirit lives on in the ways that matter most: through the memories and stories we leave behind, through the love we shared with others, through the giant gestures and grand plans we made happen, in all the small moments when we affected someone positively and never even knew. It's the memory of us that lingers in the smell of the pie we baked every Thanksgiving. It's the story our kids tell of that time Mommy got so upset she flushed Wylie's churro down the toilet (a tale for another day, perhaps); it's the song we sang as they drifted to sleep.

We stay alive in a million small ways in people's hearts and minds, ways we are more than likely blind to day-to-day but that slowly add up to the Story—the one that echoes long after we're gone and keeps alive who we were, the words that eventually wear down after years of reciting them, until all that remains is the feeling of what was once us, once ours.

For me, as a witch, that's the gift, the reward, the shining castle on the hill: to live a life right now, this second, that leaves an imprint on this earth that can be cherished and held close by those I loved, so that when I am no longer physically here, someone can say, "She made a difference to me." If over time all I leave is a faint feeling of something, please let it be of love.

I don't need prayer to release me from all the mistakes I have made, I need no intervention to help me make it to a cloudy place filled with harp-playing cherubs. My mistakes are mine to live with and try to make up for. I walk with them every day, and every day I create my own prayer of redemption as I move through the world and try to do better. I can only hope what is left in my wake is more hope than fear, more love than hate. In the end, my children and the legacy they, in turn, leave behind will be my reward. So perhaps I do have cherubs; mine just aren't quite as angelic as the ones on the prayer cards.

Answers that are true don't come easily. It was a difficult transition to go from having all the answers defined for me to what seems a never-ending list of questions. I have had to make peace with the mystery of it all, to learn to enjoy the journey and keep my heart open. I have learned that sometimes I find my answers when I least expect to. I can read a library's worth of books, and one brief passage will stand out and ring true. Sometimes it's a bit of an overheard conversation that will send me reeling, or inspiration found in a snippet of song. Sometimes I stand in a cold, windswept Texas graveyard and suddenly know in my heart what I believe will happen when I die:

I'll go on a road trip.

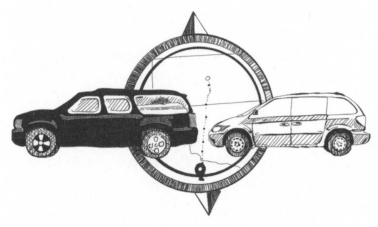

My cousin Kathy ran toward me in the parking lot, panic and bemusement chasing each other across her face.

"Find a place to park your car, for a couple days at least. You're coming with us."

What?

"They're driving her to Texas."

Driving whom? Who's driving?

"Nana. Our *parents*."

My paternal grandmother had recently died, and my aunt and father had gotten it into their heads that my grandmother should be buried next to my grandfather on his birthday—admittedly a sweet and romantic idea—and a plan had been put into motion. As far as I could see, this plan had only two flaws: my grandfather was buried two states away, and his birthday was the next day.

It had been decided that the only way to make this a reality was to take her there ourselves. I'd like to say that we were all on the same page regarding the inherent absurdity of this plan, that everyone involved understood we were boarding the crazy train. But that was ardently not the case. To my father and aunt, this seemed a completely logical turn of events.

One might ask, I daresay, how one gets a recently deceased woman across state lines to be buried beside her one true love in less than twelve hours. One might actually assume local authorities would, say, discourage a flight of fancy of this sort—and one wouldn't be entirely wrong. However, in the hours it had taken me to drive from Kansas City back to my hometown of Salina, Kansas, on hearing the news of my grandmother's death, papers had been filed and the back of my father's Chevy Suburban had been carefully measured. When I arrived, they were already stamped, loaded, and ready to go. This was really happening.

And so it went—my uncle Phil, my mother, my cousin Kathy, and I drove in one car, while my father, my aunt Judy, and my dead grandmother rode in the other. We headed south toward Texas as the sun began to set over the endless winter fields of Kansas. As we drove down the dusky highway, it became clear that despite the measurements, we might very well be pushing the Suburban's carrying capacity. Any change in the vehicle's speed pushed the coffin against the back door, causing the interior dome light to turn on, shining what felt like a spotlight on our rather unusual cargo. Soon we had a regular routine developed around stopping to push Nana farther in and shut the tailgate tight once again.

It stopped being odd after the first couple times. Of course it did.

In fact, after the first couple times, my uncle Phil began to take a bit of joy in shining his brights on my father as he shoved the coffin, flowers sliding off the polished top, back into the truck. I wonder to this day if some other family has a story they tell of the time they saw what looked like a coffin sliding out of a Chevy Suburban on I-35 late one winter's night.

But aside from the obvious, it really was very much a typical family road trip. People stopped too often to go to the bathroom. No one could agree as to what speed the caravan should be going, nor when would be a good time to stop to get something to eat. We eventually stopped at a roadside McDonald's, my Uncle Phil ordering an extra cheeseburger for "our nana waiting in the car."

The highway south through Oklahoma is a desolate one, a straight line running through occasional small towns and lonely gas stations. The skies stretched wide above us, and during our sporadic stops to push Nana back inside and re-close the back door of the Suburban, it seemed every star in the galaxy was witnessing our small clan on its sacred mission. Despite our determination to keep going, eventually we had to stop for the night. My father and aunt spent most of the night in the parking lot, making sure our grandmother continued to rest in peace undisturbed. (It was decided taking the coffin into the hotel was possibly a bridge too far, and eventually I stopped arguing over whether anyone would actually ever steal a truck *with a coffin in the back*.)

The next morning, as the sun rose above the frozen fields of southern Oklahoma, our family was gathering in Texas, awaiting our arrival, and things felt almost normal again. We had survived the worst of it and were eager to deliver our precious cargo and reunite with our people. It was time to get to the funeral.

The graveyard was in the middle of nowhere down a small dirt road, and in the last dregs of winter it was both peaceful and unbelievably barren. It was cold and quiet and a bit lonely there—even with all of us crowded under the big white tent someone had set up for us. It was a place for endings, is the best way I can describe it, and that hit me straight in the gut. While the preacher spoke about new beginnings and the hopeful future in which we would see my grandmother again, I couldn't help but feel like this was a good-bye that was final.

I realized I wasn't willing to hedge my bets on something coming along after this. I wasn't going to assume I'd get more time in the afterlife with these crazy people—this amazing, heartfelt, determinedly insane group of people. I wasn't going to get a second chance at this life. If I was lucky, someday people who loved me might be willing to drive across the plains through a cold winter's night to deliver my body to the place they felt it should rest. *If* I was lucky. How lovely to think this life might all be just a practice run, but I was no longer able to take that gamble.

Standing in that cold, wind-blown cemetery, my beliefs were cemented. I wanted—needed—to live my life believing *this* was my one and only shot, my chance to make good decisions and fulfill my responsibility to live with and try to make up for the bad ones. I had to believe that someday, I'd have one final road trip, and that's all it would be: one final road trip. Odds were, even that would be taken without *me*; whatever was left of what I am now might bounce around in a coffin in the back of a truck, or fly on the wind in a million microscopic pieces once I met my end.

I wouldn't ask for more than that. One final road trip feels like a pretty good deal.

In my heart, I truly believe this is how it is. I wasn't always as sure as I am now, and honestly, I don't believe I ever will be completely sure. Who of us truly can be? I've just found an answer that makes living this crazy life a little easier for me to bear. It gives my heart a kind of peace I never had before about how I choose to live. Whether what I believe is actually the case, well, we'll all eventually find out. Until then, I will live as if this is all I will be given and hope I'm doing okay.

My truth, however, isn't necessarily every Wiccan's belief. As with so much in Wicca, the number of theories and thoughts about the afterlife probably equals the number of witches themselves. Many people I know found their own truth within an existing system. Reincarnation is a popular belief, the idea that you return surrounded by the same core group of souls through every lifetime, over and over. In addition, while a good portion of Wiccans believe in reincarnation, others believe in Summerland. (Some Wiccans believe in both.) Summerland is similar to heaven in many ways, though there is no bar of behavior to meet for entrance into Summerland; even the souls of the wicked are admitted. Among those who believe in reincarnation, it is sometimes said to be a place of rest between earthly incarnations, providing a place to reflect on all you learned in your life and choose what you may need to experience in the next life—yes, some believe you actually get to have a say in what is to come, just not the details—so that with each incarnation you can strive to do better, to learn more, to help more, and to be more.

For others, who don't believe in reincarnation, Summerland is a sort of Wiccan Shangri-La, though it's different for every person. There you are reunited with those who have gone before you, and you can watch over those you left behind. The general idea is that once you have learned all you need and have lived the full gamut of emotional experiences, you can stay in Summerland for eternity.

Regardless of these differences, all Wiccans simply believe we have a place on the wheel. Where that wheel ends, where each of us stops in the spinning and what that means, well, that's up to each witch to figure out.

Often, that's no simple task. For some Wiccans, research is the path to peace, while others form their ideas purely through discussion. I often find those of us who have broken away from organized belief can be a bit annoying to everyone else: we're drowning in curiosity and overflowing with questions. Yet the process of asking those questions and stumbling upon my own answers (as well as learning to make peace with the unknown) has made the ground beneath my feet feel steadier—somehow now I feel more substantial and resilient than I ever felt simply accepting the answers someone handed down to people like me lifetimes ago.

SEEKING FORGIVENESS

I remember, as a child, sitting in the pews of a quiet church early in the morning, waiting my turn to confess my sins. I was always terrified. I would stare at the Virgin Mary, resolute before Gabriel, and say a million apologies to her before I ever reached the confessional.

It was supposed to make me feel better, this chance to have all I had done wrong immediately forgiven. I would say my prayer and list out all my misdeeds. I'd slowly count them out on my fingers. I felt like there must be a perfect number of sins, one that showed I was really trying but still acknowledged that I could never be perfect. I eventually settled on between six and eight, and I remember consciously making sure I had transgressions enough for each designated finger. One hand of sins weirdly felt like not enough, but two hands full seemed like way too many. Even so, I always feared if I had too many sin-free fingers left over, the priest would know that I wasn't listing all my sins, or that I was obviously forgetting a truly important transgression or two. Was that an even greater offense, to completely forget a sin? I didn't know, but it felt like it might be. And so I sat, listing every possible transgression, no matter how small, and steeling myself for my inevitable punishment.

My penance was never much, despite my fears to the contrary. I would be assigned an apology to someone, a handful of Our Fathers, perhaps a full rosary. (Man, the rosaries killed me. I always felt so bad when we had to bring Mary into it—I felt like she had dealt with enough, and the idea of disappointing her was always particularly heartbreaking to my small soul.)

Yet, once I was finished confessing and doing my penance, I never felt any different. I realized, years later, that this was because confession felt like a process outside myself. Someone else was judging my behavior and deciding how I could make things right, but that isn't how restitution works. I needed to truly feel remorse and do what I felt was necessary to atone for my actions—and oftentimes, atonement is not as simple as saying a rosary or offering an apology. Sometimes, sadly, I cannot make up for what I did that was wrong; I just have to try to do better next time. That hurts, but it's true: I have to live with my mistakes, with the consequences of my choices.

I'm okay with that—I'm learning to be. I have to be. I don't always honor the divine in those who surround me; sometimes I do a rather horrible job of it. I must then own up to it and make it right as much as I can. I alone carry the weight of my decisions and their consequences.

If there's no one judging our behavior for ultimate reward or punishment, no one outside ourselves to tell us what is right, you might wonder why Wiccans bother to do good at all. The answer is Wiccans believe that what you put out into this world is what will come back to you. This is often referred to as the "Rule of Three." It is most easily explained as a belief that what you send out into the world returns to you threefold. While some people may think of this as karma, it is slightly different. I believe it's meant to remind us that if we bring as much light as we can to the world, we will be more likely to receive light. Joy begets joy. If someone lives a life full of anger and negative energy, that person will most likely not be able to see past it to find the happiness that's abundant in the world. Worse, negative energy attracts negative energy, so it simply multiplies endlessly. "Misery loves company," anyone? We each define our own experience, and if we spend our experience looking to create magic and joy, we will find it many times over. If we hang on to resentment and disappointment, that's all we will ever hold.

I'm a witch. I answer to no one but myself. It is up to me to create an existence that fulfills me, that makes me happy. I fully understand the power of words and intention, and I have promised to do no harm. I am bound by my actions and deeds. That's truly what being Wiccan, being a witch, is about for me: honoring the power around me and within me, living n harmony with the world I am part of and striving to make it a better place.

For a lot of people, the definite lack of palmistry, magic wands, and incantations at the center of Wicca is a bit disappointing. Yet all of those things can be part of a given witch's practice; if you came to visit me, you would see a broom hanging on my wall, white sage in a metal bowl by my door, and a deck of tarot cards in a hand-carved wooden box at the head of my bed. Those things just aren't the heart of what being Wiccan is all about. In many ways, they are but trinkets and toys in comparison to the real work.

The real work is about taking responsibility. It's about putting in the effort to understand yourself and what you have to bring to the world. It's about honoring the divine in every living thing—not just the cute ones, not just the nice ones, but *all* living things. It's about finding a way to view those around you as part of the entirety of your experience, learning to empathize, and, yes, sometimes learning to back away slowly.

Wicca is not about spells to fix your problems but about being willing to face those problems head-on with the intention of overcoming them. It's not about changing the course of the wind so much as finding the strength to stand in it. It's not about seeking some greater power outside yourself for what you need but about finding that power within you.

It may sound hokey, but when you act with the intention to bring joy and light into the world and you trust the power you hold within yourself, you can create a spell more powerful than any love potion.

A RESTLESS SPIRIT ON AN ENDLESS FLIGHT

DISCOVERING MY IDENTITY AS A WITCH

I FIND WHEN I PRACTICE MAGIC—WHEN I FOCUS MY INTENTION FOR a greater good or outcome—more often than not, my purposes are family-focused. I am incredibly family- and home-centric. My definitions of what is home and who is family may at times be somewhat untraditional, but it is within those confines that I feel I have the most power to create good. In witchy terms, that makes me most similar to a cottage witch: someone who finds her greatest intentions enacted within her home, for her family. A cottage witch considers his or her home to be the most sacred space. Cottage witches are caretakers and homemakers, and they employ these skills to strengthen and impart their personal divine abilities.

As you can imagine, there are all kinds of witches. The cottage witch is most similar to the kitchen witch, for obvious reasons. Whereas the cottage witch incorporates sacred rituals throughout the home, the kitchen witch's focus is specifically on (you guessed it!) the kitchen. Meals are op-portunities to create with intent, to infuse meaning into every dish, every gathering. Ingredients are specifically chosen, meals carefully planned. Sigils (symbols that invoke certain kinds of power) are stirred into soups, traced out with a spoon in pancake batter. Kitchen witches find their great-est peace and comfort in the rituals of preparing food and channel their intentions in that way. Often, kitchen witches are also healers, drawing upon the natural properties of plants and herbs to help ameliorate physical and psychological ailments.

There are also practitioners called green witches. Green witches share some similarities to kitchen witches, as they, too, are often seen as healers. Green witches are what I imagine a lot of people associate with Wicca; they feel most closely connected with nature and organic elements. While all witches align themselves with the natural world, its seasons and rhythms, the green witch feels most connected to the greater universal power as it's found outdoors. Green witches often find their acts of intention tied to trees, herbs, plants, flowers, and stones. They may find grounding and inspiration in Druidic tree adulation, the Gallic sacred groves, and the practices of traditional Italian witches. (The Italian witch is historically known for "folk botany" and was often a community's healer as well.)

Sea, or water, witches are innately similar to green witches, only they find their connection to the divine power in nature through water rather than the earth. Their sacred spaces will often be lakes, rivers, or the sea, and their intentional acts or spells will more often than not have a liquid element. Due to their close association with water, they will also be especially cognizant of the tides and hold high honor for the moon. The tools they use are more likely to be found objects, such as shells for bowls, sea glass, driftwood, and sand. Sea witches have often borne the brunt of evil-witch lore—from sirens to underwater beasts, the sea witch overall gets a pretty bad rap. In reality, the sea witch is one who is often hyperaware of balance, conscious of the ever-changing motion of life. She stands on land, with her heart in the sea.

Another witch who understands duality and the precarious nature of balance is the hedge witch, so named for the hedges that once separated properties. Hedge witches feel most spiritually connected to matters of the mind and spiritual planes. Just as a hedge would stand between two properties, hedge witches stand between two worlds. They are interested in the connection between the mind and body, the physical world and the soul, and the delineation between this world and the next. Hedge witches are often closely associated with shamans; they sometimes employ similar techniques, such as drumming and meditation, to induce transformed states of awareness and to better explore alternate planes of existence. They are seen, more often than not, as possessors of great wisdom, people who are able to see the totality of existence and therefore lend guidance.

They aren't the only ones looking at the totality of things, however. Probably the most common type of witch is the eclectic witch, one who takes bits from all kinds of other practices to form his or her own path. Eclectic witches pull from various customs, traditions, and myths to establish their own unique set of rituals. Some practitioners warn against this method, which they see as simply an unwillingness to learn enough about any one path, but all in all, it's simply a way for a witch to evolve her practice as she personally evolves through time. Eclecticism is beneficial, not because a witch isn't dedicated to truly understanding what he or she is doing but rather because following a set definition of who one is and how one should practice is simply too confining.

Like seekers on any other religious path, witches find a practice that speaks to their hearts and build around that, be it a set of predefined rituals, or customs slowly collected over time. The list of witches above contains just a few basic examples; no two witches are the same. There are numerous buckets and classifications, and it seems we all pick and choose from one or two (or all) at one point or another.

As I grow in my practice and as a person, my places of power shift accordingly. In my life now, I am a mother and a wife. I find these roles to be incredibly fulfilling and empowering. Embodying those roles in my life to the best of my ability is my absolute priority. It makes perfect sense that in the here and now, I am able to harness my energy and intent most effectively in my home, around the needs of my family. Perhaps someday, when steel and stone do not surround me, I will find a greater everyday connection to soil and stars. The beauty of Wicca is I don't have to know or decide right now. My practice can ebb and grow as I do.

It might seem counterintuitive, in fact, that I belong to a religious order that is so closely tied to nature when I choose to live in one of the largest cities in the world—and not just on the outskirts, where small private patches of land exist, but right smack in the center. I admit that when I first moved to the city, well over a decade ago, I had a passing thought that I wouldn't be able to practice here in any meaningful way. I couldn't imagine heading to Central Park at dusk to try to catch a faint glimpse of a star, or walking to the West Side Highway and standing amid the exhaust trails of cars to see the setting sun. I had been spoiled thus far in my practice; living among the wild endless fields of Kansas I had always had space and ample nature available. I knew what it felt like to watch storms roll over the horizon, or to drive small two-lane roads along winding pathways with no destination in mind, just the top down and the wind waving. It was easy to connect with the universal divine power where I lived, easy to picture the wheel of life when you're in the midst of what we all associate with it: grass and sky, birds and squirrels. In New York City, even when I found nature, it was highly manufactured. I wasn't sure what to do with that.

I first fell in love with New York City in college, after a road trip with a group of friends over Valentine's Day in 1998. It was love at first sight: the energy, the art, the people. A couple years into my career, I spent six weeks commuting between my Kansas home and a client's office in Manhattan, and my heart eventually just couldn't take it anymore. I knew where I had to be. I had to *try*. When I was given the opportunity, in 2001, to study for my master's degree at Pratt Institute, I jumped at the chance. I fixed up my house, sold everything I had, and landed in the heart of Kips Bay, New York. (It wasn't until over a year later, when Sam and I had been dating long distance for some six months, that I realized how much it had become my home. I couldn't bear to depart, and so he arrived.)

Yet my first months in the city weren't easy. There was many a lonely, frightened, tear-filled night followed by a challenging day. It was the first time I was really on my own, building a home and starting anew in my career. My life felt a bit in pieces, and I struggled for some grounding.

I moved to the city at the beginning of July, so my first real Wiccan holiday here was Lammas, the first of the harvest festivals. Coming from Kansas, this holiday always felt very much like home to me. It is a time to celebrate the bounty the summer has given, the tall wheat and burgeoning gardens. In my previous life, you would find me driving small, winding roads with the top down on my convertible, surrounded by the endless wheat fields of the place I was born. I would often return home that evening to finish off the loaf of bread I had baked in my kitchen, enjoying a nice hunk of it on my back porch beneath my giant fir tree.

All that I had left behind in Kansas was as unreal as a dream once I looked around my newly acquired ten-by-sixteen-foot studio apartment. I had no idea where to begin. I peeked out my windows and saw nothing but the buildings across the street. There was no harvest here. I was at a loss for where even to begin. Just when I was finally feeling steady on my spiritual feet, so to speak, it seemed they had been swept out from under me again.

I took a halfhearted walk to Central Park. I freely admit that I did more wallowing than celebrating; I came home no more refreshed and connected than when I left. I walked to the corner grocery and bought some bread, preparing for my little lonely Lammas feast. I was in full pity-party mode. I sat on my couch in my tiny apartment and wondered if I'd ever be able to really practice Wicca in my new home.

Looking back now, I can see that a lot of what I was feeling had little to do with not knowing how to practice and everything to do with being incredibly homesick. I had no friends whom I felt comfortable inviting to help me celebrate my little pagan holiday, and the loneliness was hitting me particularly hard. I eventually gave in to tradition and decided I needed to at least try to celebrate outside, even if it was on my tarpaper roof instead of a wide expanse of grass. I packed up a little bag of bread and wine and an old blanket and headed up the two grungy flights of stairs that separated me from the topline of the city. I tiptoed past the final apartment in the building, inhabited by an old Greek man who adored regaling me with stories of his adventures with the hookers of the Upper East Side, and carefully opened the steel door to the roof, ignoring its warning about an alarm that I knew had been disconnected long ago.

In a perfect story, I would open the door to be greeted by a fresh wind that would remind me of home and a canopy of stars—but this was Kips Bay, Manhattan, and all that greeted me was a somewhat stale smell I was sure emanated from the Greek man's apartment below me, and a perfectly dark sky. What the view may have lacked in stars, however, was made up for in skyline. Above me soared the Empire State Building in its full glory, with a collection of other brightly lit buildings clamoring for attention at its feet.

I stood for a minute, taking it all in. I had spent the past month unpacking and interviewing for jobs and going to classes and trying to read subway maps and, in general, completely forgetting I was in the midst of millions of people. In all my rushing around, I had somehow left behind the girl who had visited this place years ago and sworn she would be back to stay. I had forgotten sitting on a bench in Bryant Park watching the people go by and promising myself that someday that park would be my backyard, that those people would be my neighbors.

I had entirely forgotten the spell that had originally brought me here: the small promise made to myself, the words uttered over worn postcards stuffed into favorite books, the subway token I had kept close in my wallet. I was so busy running through my everyday life, I had left my heart behind.

Suddenly, all of that overwhelmed me. Here I was, standing on my roof in the shadow of the Empire State Building, in what was now my city. I looked across at the lights and buildings and thought of all the other people sharing this night with me. I thought of all the people who were, at this very moment, starting on their journeys toward their dreams. I sat and drank my wine and ate my bread and celebrated a different kind of harvest, a different abundance. I raised my glass to millions of hopes and dreams being fulfilled that night. I sat on that sticky, somewhat smelly roof and I gave thanks for all that I had—old-Greek-man stories and all.

I realized I didn't need a forest or a field to feel connected to a divine power. I was in the midst of the divine power here, surrounded by it. The city pulsed with it: centuries of dream chasers and homebuilders, sycophants and stars, writers and artists, immigrants from foreign shores and dreamers like me. All like me. The lights in those buildings were suddenly all the stars I needed. I took a deep breath and reached out with all I had, to the soil deep beneath the buildings and streets and tunnels, to the heart that beat under it all, holding us all up. I reached out for the millions of hearts and minds that now populated my space like so many stars. I reveled in all that had come before, in the centuries of footsteps on the sidewalks, the echoes of voices all clamoring for something more.

I suddenly felt part of something great, something powerful and wonderful and revolutionary. I felt something I truly believe is part and parcel of this place: energy beyond just cars and deadlines and curtain rises and stock markets, a hopefulness and a yearning, a belief in better things to come. There was a sense of history here, a vitality that remained constant as you looked backward through the years, a promise that something great lay ahead.

It might not have been the way I was used to practicing, but it was there nonetheless. In the years to come, I spent many a night under the moon up on that roof, watching a city that very much felt like its own dynamic organism, knowing I was as much a participant in it as an observer. Reminding myself that I was one of millions here in this small place making a home, making a life—one of countless people who had done so throughout history—helped me feel my place on the wheel as much as any field or forest might have.

I still, from time to time, close my eyes as I stand on a busy street corner—the wind blowing my hair back—and think of where I grew up, of the land that shaped me. The yearning to return there no longer haunts me, however, and the feeling of having lost something vital to my spirituality has long since left. I have found a new kind of connection with the divine, and when nature calls to me I have my sacred spaces to find it, all the more sacred for their scarcity. I can sit in the community garden on our street watching the magnolia blossoms fall and commune with the great tree that survives here just as I do: roots deep, spirit pointed to the sky.

Like most things about finding my way as a witch, when I moved to the city, it took a little searching and stumbling to find the practice I needed most. Every time, however—every single time—at the end of my searching and stumbling I have found myself in a place where I feel stronger, better, happier. When I open myself up to exploring what's right for me, and not just sticking to what's been dictated from some book or a preconceived assumption, I find myself exactly where I need to be. These towers of steel and streets of stone are my home, and they have given me strength just as the trees growing tall through the cracks in the sidewalk give me hope.

For the most part, I have never thought twice about sharing my spiritual practice with strangers or acquaintances when the conversation arose. I admit I may even have taken a special kind of glee in doing so at times when I knew it would be slightly provocative. Overall, however, it was just a part of who I was and how I lived my life. Very rarely would it come up, and when it did, I never hesitated to discuss it openly. It led to many wonderful conversations with people who were eager to learn about my beliefs and share their own, and every once in a great while, it shut down a conversation with someone whose judgment I was probably better off without anyway.

But I never officially "came out" as a witch. There was no big announcement, no serious conversation with my parents over tea and cake. I never really felt like it was warranted. It was simply something personal I had decided, and then I lived my decision. Those were the days before social media, of course, before news that would otherwise go without notice was spread instantaneously across state lines. Nowadays, it would be hard not to know I'm a witch unless you truly weren't paying attention. I love to share my holidays; I write posts every Sabbat and invite friends for every feast.

That's not to say I didn't tell my parents about my newfound spiritual truth—but I did it through a number of smaller conversations. When I left the Catholic Church, I explained why I wasn't going to mass each week anymore. There followed quite a few Christmases when it was explained to me how important it was to one parent or the other that I attend midnight mass. So I did, and there I would sit, the moon high above me and choral carols swirling around me as I desperately tried to discern the line between attending and participating, between being respectful and being dishonest.

I finally decided being honest and respectful, and honoring myself and my own beliefs, mattered more than a tradition rooted in a faith I no longer held. I stopped attending midnight mass. My journey wasn't as simple as a declaration; rather, it was the walk down the winding road of finding the respect for myself to trust my heart and follow my beliefs fully.

That's not to say my transition to refusing to dishonor my own beliefs was an easy path. As we all know, finding strength in your own self, having your faith turned inward rather than outward, is the hardest thing a lot of us will ever do. I also found that letting go of certain traditions was often as hard as letting go of the beliefs that went with them. Dinners and masses and holidays were all entrenched within one another. The connections were never straight lines; they were tendrils, threads so connected it felt impossible to pull one and not have the whole bundle fall to pieces.

I tried very hard to find the right threads to pull, agonizing over how to save the strings that meant something to me and let go of the ones that were tied too closely to things that just didn't feel right anymore. I'm an only child, and I know it must have been hard on my parents to let go of some of those traditions as well, but we managed. We still have cinnamon rolls and hot chocolate if we're together at the holidays, just not at two a.m. after mass. In the end, I found ways to keep a lot of the traditions I loved and, one by one, I said good-bye to the ones I could no longer truly honor. It was an arduous process at times, and a sad one. It was these traditions, after all, that helped make me the person I am. I eventually realized, however, that setting them aside for something that felt more true to who I wanted to be wasn't abandonment—it was growth. I wasn't shunning anything or anyone. I was simply taking care of me.

Slowly, I changed the way I celebrated life's events, the way I recognized the passage of time. I did so as respectfully as I could, to myself as well as to those around me. I'd like to think I did okay.

However, as I said before, those were the days before social media, when familial gossip was reserved for truly the most interesting and controversial of topics. My own quiet path wasn't really worth talking about. It affected no one but those absolutely closest to me, and even then, it affected their lives very little and only in very pointed ways. I was never part of a giant family who got together and shared holidays and remained innately close. The occasional letters and cards circulated, but overall, we were spread to the winds, with little ever drawing us to one place. The small handful of family members I was closest with crossed the distance via occasional phone calls, birthday cards, and rare emails. When we chatted and talked, I had complete control over how much I shared. Over the phone, they couldn't see the pentacle on my wall or the talisman around my neck. The holiday feasts I spent hours cooking were too far away for invitation, too remote to be worthy of mentioning. None of it, really, was worth mentioning.

At least that's what I told myself.

That was precisely how I avoided talking about my new spiritual path with the one person I was most terrified to tell—until the day came when I couldn't put it off anymore.

THAT'S THE POWER MAKES
THE WORLD GO ROUND

M A R R I A G E   A N D   W I C C A

SAM PROPOSED TO ME ON A CHILLY NIGHT IN NOVEMBER. WE WERE under a grove of trees lit up with tiny white lights in the courtyard of Tavern on the Green. It was incredibly romantic and not at all as traditional as it sounds. He stood with me, holding my hands and saying amazing things about us being partners in crime for the rest of our lives, while I distractedly gazed at the wedding reception that was taking place in the Crystal Room just across the way. It was only when I took my eyes off the myriad wedding guests, interrupting Sam's unappreciated yet lovely monologue to exclaim, "They're playing Kenny Rogers!" that I saw the small wooden box in his hand. (Look, what can I say? I was *not* expecting a proposal. *And it was Kenny Rogers!*)

He said all the nice things again, standing firmly on both feet. I didn't cry; there were no tears running down my cheeks as I said yes. There were none of the things that seem to be standard when it comes to marriage proposals. It was just him and me, under the stars in Central Park, choosing each other to the strains of "Through the Years."

It was unbelievably perfect.

While Sam was ready to catch a cab straight to city hall the next morning, I had dreams of an October wedding. I couldn't imagine a better time of year to make those kinds of promises: a time when the earth was clothed in her most beautiful colors and the world stopped for a bit, ready to begin what is, according to the precepts of Wicca, a new year. It felt right to start our new life together then, and after a bit of persuading, we set a date for the Saturday closest to Halloween.

The next year was filled with invitations and playlists and venues and budgets and paper leaves. It was filled with infinite numbers of poems and fabric swatches, documents packed with photos of bouquets and cupcakes, all the things that slowly but surely fill your days when planning a wedding.

Sam and I had promised each other that come what may, this wedding would be about us, first and foremost, and what we wanted. There would be no apologies for not following anyone else's traditions. There would be no apologies for who we were. I was a witch and he was, well, Sam. We would do this on our terms. We planned each detail so it reflected who we were, separately as well as together. We talked about what was most important to us: We wanted it to be joyous. We wanted it to be celebratory. We wanted the ceremony to reflect who we were and what we believed in, without all the trappings of a traditional rite.

We started researching pagan wedding ceremonies.

A lot of people believe Wicca is a feminist spiritual path, that it revolves around women and the male counterpart is relegated. That isn't altogether true. What's true is that Wicca offers up the idea that we all, men *and* women, hold inside of us the power that is usually held only for our gods, that we are a part of a greater world and the power that goes with it. We have the ability to draw from the strength of trees, the force of the wind, the determination of the mountain stream. We are connected to all of it and have a part to play. Neither one is greater: male or female, masculine or feminine. In fact, it is grandly acknowledged and celebrated in Wicca that the greatest divine creative power is accessed when the two meet, creating balance in body and mind, physical and spiritual, intent and action. The inner and outer worlds, our physical world as well as the collective unconscious, the zeitgeist: it's all a careful balancing act. It's a matter of recognizing all there is and finding a place within it. Wicca asks that we strive to live whole lives, kind and informed and connected lives, and that we claim responsibility for them.

When Sam and I were ready to be married, that was one of the larger themes we wanted to emphasize: balance. We chose to be married October 29th, the nearest Saturday to Samhain, when the world sits poised at the edge of summer and winter, light and dark, warm and cold. We held the ceremony at sunset, when the world was between the sun and the moon. As part of our service, we had a wreath ceremony, a common ritual in pagan handfastings. The foundation of the wreath is oak and ivy—oak is symbolic of the god, ivy represents the goddess. The two natural elements are intertwined, but neither is reliant on the other—they exist in perfect balance.

As our wreath was hung, our best man and matron of honor read these words: "The wreath has been created from ivy, a traditional symbol of matrimony and friendship. The circular shape of the wreath mirrors the rings that Sam and Misty will exchange and symbolizes the never-ending devotion that they pledge each other on this day. Ivy does not feed the tree it clings to, and this is important to its symbolism today. Nothing can separate ivy from a tree it has once embraced, and if the tree falls, the ivy stays around it. But the ivy is held to the soil by its own roots. It gets nothing from the substance of the companion, and though it dies on the same spot, it dies in its own time, making its own independent gesture. Today, Sam and Misty have cemented the bond that they share but they have not ceased to grow as individuals."

It was a reminder that is dear to me to this day. We are our strongest when we come together not as one being or one mind and point of view but as two individuals—separate beings. We each have power in our own right, and what makes our strength together truly remarkable is that we choose each other. We do so not out of need or lack of fulfillment, but having made a decision that we prefer to walk this path with the other by our side as god and goddess, as friend and lover.

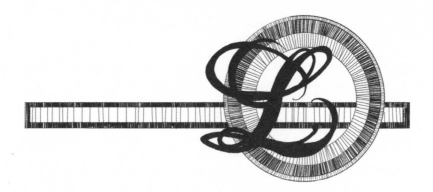

As we were making our plans, from time to time, I would get a phone call or an email from my aunt Judy, asking me about a certain aspect of the celebration, and every time a piece of my heart caught in my throat. I would answer only in general terms, sharing the what or the when but not the why. I told a lot of half-truths. I had decided I couldn't share all the things I wanted to with Aunt Judy, for fear she wouldn't come. Silently, I had already begun trying to make peace with the fact that my wedding might be the last time I saw her.

Judith Anne Thibodeaux was a force of nature—probably the first woman I ever saw that way. From my very earliest memories, she stayed in my mind as at once beautiful and proper, and not to be trifled with. She was one of those people who commanded the room simply by being in it. She seemed to me the quintessential Southern woman: loving, kind, and mannered while still somehow being fierce, loyal, and formidable.

She also had an uncanny way of making me feel absolutely beyond loved. She was my father's older sister, and while I was never close to my grandmother, I gravitated toward my aunt Judy. She always made me feel like the most special girl in the room. She could do that, could make you feel that no matter what else was happening, she *saw* you. She recognized you, saw that you mattered. She did that for me from the very start, and I adored her for it.

One of my earlier memories is of receiving a giant box from her on the Easter of my First Communion. It seemed at the time to be as big as my seven-year-old self. It was a giant white box with her scripted handwriting running across the top: *Miss Misty Lee Bell*. It was just for me. I remember feeling so grown up, so special, so completely cherished.

When I tore open the top of the box, I was greeted with mountains of white tissue paper, all printed with tiny gold flowers. Hidden amongst the folds and crinkles of those never-ending sheer paper clouds were small, individually wrapped presents—a literal treasure trove. Each precisely wrapped item held a special note, and as I carefully and excitedly tore the Scotch tape and peeled back the tissue on each one, I could not have felt more prized. I cannot tell you, sadly, exactly what all that box contained; my memories of the items themselves are a bit blurry. What I can tell you is what her handwriting looked like when she wrote *God bless you!* and *Congratulations!*, how the *L* in my middle name looped in a way that I tried to emulate in page after page of my Big Chief notebook for months afterward. I can tell you that I still think back to how that giant box of handwritten notes and tissue-wrapped packages made me feel, and that I still strive to make the people I love feel as loved as I felt in that moment. That was her gift, creating moments that made you feel extraordinary.

There was a long time, between the tilting end of my childhood and my young adulthood, when I lost contact with my aunt Judy. Politics and drama among the adults in my family kept her letters and packages away for years at a time and made me hide away in a corner for far too long once I was old enough to reach out on my own. I thought perhaps I wasn't welcome after such a prolonged absence. I feared picking sides. I feared *not* picking sides. I let my phone stay quiet and my mailbox empty of outgoing letters for years—years I should have been running in her direction.

When I look back, I am heartbroken at what those years cost me. Yet once we began to communicate again, you never would have guessed that she and I ever missed a beat. She pinched my cheeks and hugged me hard and called me by both my first and middle names as if no time had passed at all.

I had been in her heart the whole time, she said to me every time I tried to apologize. We had never really parted.

For all of that, I strove to make her proud. I would do pretty much anything to make her smile in that way that said I had done well, even though by that time I was a full-fledged adult. She adored that I dyed my hair red (the same color hers was naturally); she marveled at me moving to New York City on my own. I reveled in telling her about my friends and my work. I took great joy in telling her about my then boyfriend Sam and how I thought, just perhaps, he was the One.

I delighted in sharing my life with her, and because of that, I thought my heart would burst every time we spoke and she told me I was like her. I was terrified to point out the one big thing that made us different. Every time I came close, all that came to mind was that giant, beautiful box of tissue-wrapped items.

I still hadn't mastered that loop in my *L*.

Time passed, and I successfully avoided any outright mention of my decision to become a practicing Wiccan. In fact, over ten years went by with me quietly just avoiding the topic. I hadn't ever been ashamed of my decision before, never turned from discussing it when it came up with anyone else, but I was terrified to tell her. I was frightened that if she knew she would think less of me, that she would see me differently.

She would believe I was going to hell.

I would lose her—for good this time, and in the ways that mattered most. I just couldn't bear it.

A piece of me, though, hoped maybe my wedding day would help me show her all the things I was having a hard time saying, would help explain all the things I couldn't find words for. I wanted to show her I had built a life that made me truly happy, even though I feared the details of it would make her truly *un*happy. I dove headlong into planning.

Sam and I took a bit from here, a bit from there, and began building a wedding we felt truly reflected us, the path that brought us together, and the promises we wanted to make for the future. At last we finalized the ceremony, and I sent it out to our friends who would stand with us that day. We called Sam's aunt Kathy to help us find all the right herbs and plants for our wreath. We crouched on the floor for several nights in a row, piecing bits of silk together in a long ribbon of Morse code that spelled out *I do* for our handfasting. I ordered torches and lanterns. We sent in the paperwork to have our friend Scott ordained online, and then asked how he felt about singing Huey Lewis and the News's "The Power of Love" when he declared us man and wife.

We ordered beer and champagne. I overnighted cheesecakes.

Sam ordered more beer.

As the wedding got closer, my time was filled with last-minute errands and joyful reunions and I no longer had the spare moments to worry about what people would think when we made our promises—I was too excited to make them.

We said our vows under a small oak tree as the sun set, our hands woven together with our handmade ribbon.

"I, by the life that courses within my blood and the love that resides within my heart, take you to my hand, my heart, and my spirit—to be my chosen one. To desire and be desired by you, to possess you and be possessed by you, without sin or shame, for naught can exist in the purity of my love for you. I promise to love you wholly and completely, without restraint, in sickness and in health, in plenty and in poverty, in life and beyond, where we shall meet, remember, and love again. I shall not seek to change you in any way. I shall respect you, your beliefs, your people, and your ways as I respect myself."

We danced up the aisle and through the rest of the night.

It wasn't until a week later, when I opened my email account after such a long time away from work, that all my worries returned. They came back full force, a crashing reminder staring at me forebodingly in my Hotmail inbox. Aunt Judy had emailed me, and the subject line was *Questions*.

I stared at that line in my list of emails for entirely too long. I admit I panicked. I considered just pretending it wasn't there, that I hadn't gotten it. I played through all the possible outcomes. I took a deep breath and prepared for what could be the last time I heard from her, the last time she would *want* to say anything to me.

Then I opened it up and realized how grossly I had underestimated her.

She started off with just normal assurances—hellos and weather chat and how-are-yous. Then, in the second paragraph, she came right out and asked if I was Wiccan. There was no big buildup, no fanfare, no judgment. You see, she said, I thought your ceremony was lovely and I looked it up. It seems, from what I found, that a lot of the rituals were Wiccan. Are you Wiccan?

She looked them up.

She looked them up carefully enough to call me not just *pagan*, but *Wiccan*. She had done her homework in a major way. She had cared enough to read about what she thought I believed, and it didn't end there. She had continued to research. She asked if there were books I would recommend, which websites she could visit. She told me the ones she had already found, what she had already read. She wanted to learn more, she said.

I was floored. At that point, I had been practicing for over ten years. No one in my life, save Sam, had shown such an avid interest in understanding how I had chosen to live. People accepted it, yes, but there is a huge difference between accepting and understanding, between acknowledging and supporting. Aunt Judy didn't get upset that I didn't tell her. She didn't gloss over it or treat it like a phase. She didn't decide to just ignore it. She embraced it.

She embraced me.

I thought my heart would burst. I sat there, at my little cubicle in the middle of an open floor on the thirty-fifth floor in Midtown, and cried. Right there in front of the wall of file cabinets and the Xerox machine, I tore through a box of Kleenex all on my own.

I replied to her email later that day, but my message didn't contain any of the words it should have. It didn't tell her how it felt to be so loved, or the profound gratitude I would always hold for the small act it was for her to sit in front of Google, or in her local bookstore, reading up on pagan wedding ceremonies. I didn't tell her how much less alone I felt in our family, or how a piece of my soul that had been holding its breath had now let out a long sigh.

I could never find the right words.

I sent her some books and a couple websites. I listed the holidays. I told her about our Sabbat dinners, to which we invited our friends, and the nights I stared out our window at the moon and reminded myself I was just one of so many helping the world go round. I told her how the moon reminded me I could always start over without losing who I was. I tried to explain the basics of what I believed in my own words. I failed in a million ways in that email, and in all the ones that followed. To this day, I wish I could go back and write them all again—somehow let her know what her words meant to me, what she meant to me. Somehow answer her questions wholly and completely.

But despite my lack of words, hers continued to bolster me throughout the following decade. She never missed a solstice, never missed an equinox. She was the first, at every holiday, to wish me a merry one. She continued to research Wicca over the years, continued to ask me questions. We had our differences of belief, but she never judged me and never turned her back. She never stopped walking with me on the path I had chosen. I was always, first and foremost, her niece. She carried me in her heart.

That was the greatest gift she ever gave me—one of the greatest gifts I have ever been given, period.

I guess this book is my belated gift to her. I am finally able to find the words that failed me before. I can finally answer all of her questions.

I LIGHT A CANDLE THEN
I CALL YOUR NAME

THE GODS AND
GODDESSES, SYMBOLS,
AND TOOLS OF WICCA

So THERE ARE NO RULES IN WICCA, AND THERE'S NO OFFICIAL HEAD wizard or grand sorceress. I'm offering up none of the fun stuff, I know. *So disappointing.* I wonder myself how you and I have gotten this far into it, what with the general lack of sequined shoes and crooked noses to be discussed. Truth be told, however, I do keep a few trinkets and tools around that are delightfully and wonderfully witchy.

Objects can be useful in focusing intent, and even I fall prey, from time to time, to the delicious design of an illustrated tarot or hand-bound leather notebook. And there are some basic tools in Wicca that are handy to know about, ones that pretty much every witch employs at one time or another. Perhaps they're not as mystical as one would hope, but nonetheless, they're there. I never set out to compile a collection of magical tools, but now as I look around I realize that's exactly what I have. Just as I never purposely built an altar in my home, and yet there is one, right by our front door. As I practice what feels right to me, I gradually begin to employ items I might not otherwise own, or imbue items I already have with a very particular and often sacred meaning.

Like any religious or spiritual practice, Wicca has its own symbology that helps guide our practice and understanding. Some of the symbols have roots that go back centuries, others seem more conjured out of fairy tales; all have specific and fabled meanings. You would more than likely see them on any number of items if you were to walk into your local (witch)craft store or New Age shop. It's important to understand the significance and story of the symbols before making use of them, because they are as sacred as any other religious iconography to those who view them as symbols of devotion and reverence.

Reaching for the Stars

Key amongst these is the symbol of the earth, or life, itself: the pentacle. The most prominent symbol of our faith, it is also the most misused and misunderstood. There are endless variations of the pentacle (also called the pentagram), but they all act as a talisman of the main elements of life and our practice. Of course, this simple shape (often held within a circle) has a history that is far from simple. It has been an esoteric symbol, imbued with magical qualities, for as long as it has existed. It has carried an inordinate amount of mysticism over the years for simply being five equal lines uniting to form what we all now read as a star.

Our modern-day understanding has often misaligned the pentacle with evil: Goth girls holding hands around a circle and star etched into a wooden floor, the symbol swirling around the possessed while a priest holds a crucifix before him in protection, the flaming star turned upside down acting as some sort of portal to the netherworld. All of these images hold a tremendous amount of drama but little else. The true meaning and use of the pentacle are nowhere near its all-too-familiar contemporary presentation. As with most symbols and stories related to paganism and modern witchcraft, this presentation has little to do with actuality and a lot to do with fantasy. This time, though, I can say with absolute certainty that the real story is just as good as the fable. Our little star has had quite a run.

The use of the pentacle through time is really beautiful. It's not tied exclusively to paganism—quite the opposite. It was first seen thousands of years ago and has woven its way through various meanings and belief systems ever since. The pentacle is one of the oldest markings known to humankind, used in Mesopotamia as far back as 6000 BCE. Historians have even found the pentacle within the dictionary of Sumerian glyphs, and have surmised it may have been associated with directions: above, forward, backward, left, right.

Our little symbol wasn't confined to just the ancient Middle East, however. During this same time period, we can also find the pentacle representing the five elements of the Chinese zodiac: earth, fire, wood, water, and metal. The Egyptians associated the five-pointed star with the underground womb, from which all of life was reborn. Ancient cosmologists (astronomers who study the origin of the universe) saw it rising above them, representing the planets Jupiter, Mercury, Mars, Saturn, and Venus (the brightest and most easily visible of our nine planets). Amazingly, Venus itself spends every eight years (and five days, if you want to be exact, and why not) tracing a pentacle in the sky on the zodiacal belt. It's no wonder the pentacle is so ingrained in human imagery; it continually crosses above us in our night sky.

It seems even from our earliest days, these five connected points represented some form of elemental life and mystery to us.

Even in ancient times, however, our little symbol was associated with defiance. The ancient Greek philosopher Pythagoras used the symbol as a mark of man, the uppermost point denoting the head, with arms and legs spread wide. When his school was broken up and that tyrant of Samos, Polycrates, forced him underground, his students used the pentacle as a secret symbol to identify one another. Pythagoras is credited not just with the first use of the pentacle to subvert authority but also with helping expand the pentacle's geography. He was a well-known traveler—being banished from your homeland will do that to a person—and historians think it's possible his influence is an explanation for the pentacle's appearance in early Hindu tantric writings and art.

Time carried on, and our simple emblem of existence continued on with it. As early as approximately 300 CE, the pentacle began to make its appearance in the Abrahamic religions. In ancient Judaism, it was a symbol of truth and represented the five books of the Pentateuch. The emperor Constantine used the pentacle on his seal and amulet. Early in the Middle Ages, Christians (yes, Christians!) began to use the pentacle as way to symbolize the life of Christ, a symbol of his five wounds.

In Arthurian legend, it was the emblem of Sir Gawain, King Arthur's nephew, emblazoned on his shield in red and gold. Seen as a mark of protection, the pentacle appeared throughout the Middle Ages on jewelry, amulets, and knights' shields and battle attire. It was said to hold the five knightly virtues: generosity, courtesy, chastity, chivalry, and piety. It became a key symbol of Christianity in this period, and is noted in some texts as the prominent symbol of Christianity before the cross came into popularity.

The pentacle has a long history as a symbol of life, power, and protection that traverses pagan and Judeo-Christian histories. Unfortunately, that unified view of the symbol has long since fallen into discord. Its downfall began with fourteenth- and fifteenth-century occult practices that borrowed heavily from Judeo-Christian symbolism, and with misinformation that spread like wildfire during the witch hunts of the time. The pentacle's ecumenical origins soon became forgotten, and it began to be seen and used as a mark of evil.

The pentacle had a comeback (don't call it a comeback!) with the twentieth-century pagan revival. There are multiple theories as to why these philosophies and traditions resurfaced—a reaction to the increasing industrialization of people's lives, even the repeal of a number of Witchcraft Acts in Europe. Regardless of the impetus, old traditions were made new, and the groups practicing them adopted the pentacle as a life symbol once again. However, despite neo-pagans reclaiming the pentacle as a unifying symbol of life, they were still people who lived on the fringes of society, and in spite of their best efforts, a larger cultural influencer soon entered the scene. The newly burgeoning business of Hollywood began to use the pentacle as a shock inducer in just about every horror movie it made; the pentacle was firmly back in the wider consciousness, but for all the wrong reasons. It's really only now, in the beginning of the twenty-first century, that the misinformation about the pentacle has died down and knowledge about what it really is and what it truly means to those who associate with it has become more available, helping remove some of the stigma of this age-old icon.

In Wicca, the meaning of the pentacle is pretty simple and straightforward. And after this long history I've just harangued you with, you can see it's also nothing new. To Wiccans, the points of the star represent the five elements—earth, wind, fire, water, and spirit—enclosed in a circle representing the universe, which connects and contains them all.

I find that to be lovely, and it makes me happy to see it. I have a pentacle hanging on the wall in our living room, and it's something I find my eyes resting on from time to time. I love that it reminds me we are all connected: every living thing, every element of life. How lucky I am to get to be a part of such wonder. I admit, however, I was more than a little nervous to wear a pentacle around my neck when I first started practicing, as much as I wanted to. I was at once proud of being a witch and terrified of what some people's reaction would be. I knew well the assumptions that came with the pentacle, and I didn't want my faith to be misconstrued. My first pentacle was a small silver token of flowers woven in the star-and-circle design. It was hard, on first glance, to see what it truly was, and I felt protected when I wore it—in more ways than one.

I eventually got braver with my choices. I stopped choosing the charms that were hardest to immediately identify and started wearing the ones that truly spoke to me. There are a million designs of pentacle amulets, and finding just the right one to wear was important to me. I wanted it to represent me not just by what it was but by what it looked like.

As I became more steadfast in my beliefs, I was better able to answer the questions that can sometimes come up when you wear a symbol most people associate with evil spells and Satan worshippers. I no longer felt the need to hide the star behind intricate designs or under the collar of my shirt.

I even became able to absorb the disapproving looks I would get from the occasional passersby without it affecting my spirit.

Yes, that still happens. I hate to even say it, but it does. I have been called a "witch" by perfect strangers with a venom I am often surprised can still be associated with the word. I have been told I'm going to hell based on the presence of the pentacle around my neck, which would hurt more if I actually believed in such a place. I once was spit on as I was walking my children home from school. I choose, however, to accept that everyone has something about them that another person can find to hate. I teach my children that incidents like these are rare, and that when someone reacts so viscerally to something so innocuous, it says more about him or her than it does about you. How sad to carry so much unhappiness in you that it overflows in such a way to other people.

I find now when I wear my pentacle, a simple silver ring surrounding a clear star inscribed with the words *Life, love, liberty, all good things come to me*, it has become more rare to get negative reactions from those around me—or perhaps I have become blinder to them. I want to believe the former. I want to believe that as people we are becoming more understanding and more open to discovering our shared beliefs rather than emphasizing what divides us. I want to believe that, slowly but surely, the pentacle is gaining back its original meaning: a simple star, holding all of life and mystery in its bounds.

Holy Trinities of the Witchy Kind

You'll see other symbols rampant in various craft stores and New Age shops. Most of the others widely used in Wicca usually represent the god and/or goddess. You will frequently see the triple moon, a simple full circle with outward-facing crescents on either side to represent the waxing, full, and waning moons. These moons represent the three stages of the goddess: the maiden, mother, and crone. The maiden is the waxing moon, full of upcoming promise; the mother is the full moon, full of ripeness, power, and stability; and the crone is the waning moon, representing wisdom, tranquility, and death.

With all this symbolic weight behind it, we follow the moon in our spiritual practice closely. Its ever-evolving presence above us is unrelenting. I hear some witches even dance beneath it. I've never seen or participated in such things, but the idea seems rampant in both stories and assumptions, so I feel like it must be happening somewhere. *Anyhoo* (as my father-in-law would say), each phase of the moon is a reminder that the world spins on, no matter what small or large trivialities play out alongside. The moon disappears and grows, it pulls the tides, it builds and retreats. During the waxing moon, as the great disc grows, it is a reminder to begin new things, to explore new places, a sign to align with the natural cycle of growth and rebirth. The moon calls us to notice that there is always another chance, always another opportunity to build yourself anew.

As the moon diminishes, it signifies the time to let go of old thoughts and practices. It is a time for internal reflection, a time to contemplate who we want to be and how we can leave behind the things that are holding us back from our full potential, from living out a life as our true selves. The dark of the new moon is the time to conceptualize ideas and invoke change, the full moon a reminder to live as brightly and wholly as we can. The moon acts as a compass, a reminder that the world around us is always changing (and us with it), a reminder that we are a part of something greater, something bigger.

That we are surrounded by stars.

I love the triple-moon symbol of the goddess, as I love the moon. The never-ending cycle of promise, growth, and letting go is instrumental in reminding me to take each moment as it comes and live with intention.

In a similar symbolic vein, the triquetra, or the Celtic triple knot, is made up of one continuous line interweaving around itself, symbolizing no beginning or end. It creates a three-pointed shape, often connected by an unbroken circle. It represents many things that are perceived to come in threes: life (aesthetic, ethical, religious), time (past, present, future), and dominions (earth, sea, sky). For pagans and Wiccans specifically, it is most often linked to the goddess, much like the triple moon. However, the trinity is hardly exclusive to pagans—quite the opposite, in fact. The triquetra is another symbol that is shared with Christianity, in which it's associated with the Holy Trinity.

Because of this overlapping of meaning, the triquetra holds special significance for me personally. In many ways, it symbolizes both where I have come from and where I am going, what I was raised to believe and what I hold to be true in my heart now. For me, this simplest of the Celtic knots represents my not-so-simple journey. I hold it fast, and it repeats across many areas of my life. Variations of it hang in wooden carvings above my children's beds; silver versions of it circle my fingers; a charm of it hung from my wedding bouquet. On the right day, if you walk behind me, you'll see one peeking out from the top of my shirt collar, forever a part of me.

Not all Wiccan symbols are goddess-centric, however. Even though it is commonly thought that Wicca is goddess-based, it's truly about balance. What is the goddess without the god? We tell the tale of the god and goddess moving around the wheel of the year as it turns, the goddess growing from maiden to mother to crone as the year progresses, the god maturing from child to lover to hunter. Neither exists without the other. Some may relate, or find kinship more strongly with one or the other, but they are, above all, simply ways to frame the inexplicable power that runs through all living things. They remind us we are all on that wheel as it turns, all moving through a cycle of days: growing, learning, changing, moving forward. We are all in turn the maiden, mother, and crone; the child, lover, and hunter.

So naturally, the goddess has a consort. When searching for her other half, you find the Horned Man or Green Man. He is the god of the wild, who loves and protects the goddess and all of her children. He is the sun to her moon, the feral spirit to her nurturing one. He rises and falls through the year as well, born as the light begins to enter the world, only to die as it leaves. As some Wiccans see it, he is born from the union of the masculine and feminine, the child she brings forth every winter—the light burning bright ahead. He is her lover, marrying her in the spring; her protector, the hunter, as she grows large with child; until he falls quiet when the darkness reigns, only later to be born once again with the return of the sun. He, too, is the cycle of life, dancing through the stages of being, rising and falling with the sun.

Some believe he is dually both the Horned Man/Oak King and the Green Man/Holly King, who battle for the goddess's affections twice a year. The Horned Man is said to rule from midsummer to midwinter, when he is beaten by the Green Man and gives up his throne until they meet again at the summer solstice to once again trade places. They are seen as two sides of a coin, the one unable to exist without the other.

Regardless of the story one chooses, the symbology is the same; the god is the companion of the goddess, her other half, her balance. He is powerful and righteous on his own and is often shown as being made of the wild he represents: covered in leaves and branches, or composed of the spirits of animals, with great horns or antlers sprouting from his head. Simplified, his symbol is akin to hers; he is represented as the pure circle of the sun holding up a crescent as if it were antlers.

I find my use of the god symbols less active than my use of the goddess ones, which is simply a matter of preference and kinship. But I admit at times it's good for me to remember that even the goddess had a consort, a partner, a friend—another that balanced her. I love thinking of it that way, that the goddess has the god just as the sun has the moon, light has the dark, and winter has the summer. She is powerful in her own right and yet is able, still, to find a counterpoint. While I might not carry a traditional symbol of the god with me as I do of the goddess, I do hold his presence close. The wedding ring on my left hand is as much a representation of the god as any antlered deity.

There are myriad ways a witch might find greater meaning, consolation, or exemplification of power in these various symbols. Sometimes, like a crucifix or a Star of David, they are simply a way to express our faith. They are engraved on boards, etched on glasses, cast as jewelry. You can find them as carvings to hang on walls, bumper stickers for your car, and, as in my case, tattoos across someone's skin. And of course, there are a million symbols with sacred meaning that I have not mentioned. There are the various symbols originating from across multiple cultures that are held dear to certain practitioners, such as the Egyptian ankh (life and immortality) or the Tree of Life (a Celtic symbol of how everything from the heavens to the earth are connected). Some witches take inspiration from more natural symbology, finding themselves connected to certain animals as totems, such as the crow or owl for wisdom or the spider for power or growth. According to how he or she practices, a witch may look to any number of meaningful marks for security and influence.

The Tools of the Trade

Most often, you will find symbols sacred to a witch on the tools she uses to practice. And yes, despite my hemming and hawing about witchcraft, I, too, have instruments for my practice. There are a handful of fairly basic items most witches will have, or at least that you will find in any "So you're ready to be a witch!" kit on a shelf or list printed in a book somewhere. I'll explain what I have and how I use it, but again, if this is something that interests you, my guess is you will find what suits you best through exploration.

The first item I will mention is one that took me decades to actually obtain. I never saw a great use for it. I practiced alone, and while I kept some notes on holidays and traditions on my computer, I never really thought of that collection of notes as a spell book, or a grimoire. In actuality, that's exactly what they were, even though they were simply a folder on my virtual desktop.

A grimoire is essentially exactly what you hope it would be: a book of spells. It's a lot more than that, too, but that's the fun definition. The word itself is widely believed to have its roots in the Old French word *grammaire*, the word for books written in Latin. By the eighteenth century, though, *grammaire* referred exclusively to books of magic. Historians have postulated that the term was adapted because books of magic still circulated as Latin manuscripts at the time. I love that the word has its roots in a word I find familiar, *grammar*. It feels right that it shares meaning with a word that defines the way sentences of a language are constructed, that it references how meaningful and lasting a string of words can be.

Almost every witch ever portrayed in books or movies has a spell book, a place where she writes down the rituals she performs and how she performs them. The famous Sanderson sisters from Disney's movie *Hocus Pocus* had a grimoire with a live eyeball on the cover. A historically famous grimoire is the Book of Shadows owned by Gerald Gardner, one of the originators of modern Wicca in Britain. He claimed, in the 1940s, to have been given his "ancient magical text" by a secret coven of witches, the last in a line of ancient fertility worshippers. Due to Gardner's place in Wiccan history, the term *Book of Shadows* is now often used interchangeably with *grimoire*.

Some Wiccans have a family grimoire, passed from generation to generation, with each contributing its own small addenda. You can also buy grimoires full of prewritten spells and rituals, or blank books with fancy witchy covers. If you search "grimoire" on Amazon, you will get no less than 4,300 results, so there are plenty to be had. I myself find the prewritten books to be a bit lacking in heart, since what I practice of Wicca is so very personal, but I imagine they are a good place to start if you're wondering exactly what goes in one.

As a new and solitary practitioner, figuring out what tools work best, what books to pay attention to, and what information I wanted to leave behind was as much part of my practice as defining what I believed. Learning the methodology other Wiccans used, what their thoughts and beliefs were, played heavily into how I have come to understand and process a lot of the traditions and holidays surrounding my personal rituals. Being able to delve into variant lines of thought and custom has allowed me the freedom to pick and choose what feels right to me. In a lot of ways, I feel like because as Wiccans we're all doing that—just seeking out answers to our own personal truths—we expect no two of us will practice exactly the same, and it fosters a kind of inherent tolerance of religious belief regardless of whether or not it's pagan. When the backbone of your spiritual practice rests on the premise that there is no black or white, right or wrong, it's hard to get righteous about someone else's "right." I lived in a worldview that handed me a book that was supposed to have the answers, and as comforting as it was to have a way to cleanly define right and wrong, I find myself much more at peace now with an open book and blank pages—or, even more accurately, a somewhat jumbled list of thoughts, dreams, and questions.

Like I said earlier, my grimoire, such as it was for decades, was simply a collection of notes I kept on my computer. I didn't even think of it as an official "grimoire," just as a reference for how I had celebrated previous holidays or notes on traditions I had found that interested me in books or on websites. It wasn't until my third anniversary with Sam that he gave me a gift that later became my own Book of Shadows, one that I now use regularly and fully plan on passing on to Samaire and Wylie.

The traditional third-anniversary gift is often said to be leather. Sam and I always try to follow the symbology for each anniversary, as it requires you to be a bit creative and endow each gift with a little extra meaning. On anniversary number three, Sam gave me a leather-bound recipe book with the date of our wedding embossed across the front. Inside were the usual blank recipe cards and clear plastic pockets to keep them in. I know, right? It hardly sounds chock full of mysticism and divination. When I first received it, I never thought, "This will make a great Book of Shadows!" nor is that what Sam intended. He knew I love to cook and that I often make up my own recipes, and he wanted me to have a way of keeping them all in one place.

Soon, however, I realized I was chronicling all our special Sabbat meals, our favorite dishes. I was noting when I had made them and how I had changed the original recipes over time. I had carefully recorded our favorite recipes from each of our families growing up. I was writing down what the children ate for their first meals. I would slip in small poems I found that I loved, or notes Sam or the kids had left me. I was beginning, unintentionally, to transcribe how we chose to celebrate what was important to us. I was recording our family history in the way that suited us best: interspersed with and through the food we made and shared.

I soon found myself reaching for that recipe book every holiday, whether to use a recipe out of it or add one. It became my go-to. I remember, one Samhain, unfurling the leather tie to find our meal and realizing I had a grimoire. Each recipe told a story; each had an occasion tied to it and meaning in its ingredients. This small, now well-worn leather book holds the majority of my most oft-used and precious spells.

My Book of Shadows might look like a collection of odd and unusual recipes and random notes of memories and thoughts, but it is magical just the same. Every witch will find her own way of recording and documenting what she believes and how she lives her faith, and that, in turn, becomes her grimoire. It can be a digital folder on her hard drive, a collection of photos in an album, or, yes, even a collection of stained, handwritten recipe cards tied together by a leather string. What's important is that it's her truth in the way she feels most comfortable telling it.

A grimoire is a way to tell your story. And we all have stories to tell.

Now that we've got the spell book, we need a cauldron, right? What spell would be complete without a bubbling cauldron filled with disgusting yet intriguing ingredients? Well, truth be told, just about any spell would be good to go minus the cauldron, and yet I have a cauldron just the same. You can find them in all shapes and sizes, depending on what the witch wants to use it for. Mine is a small metal bowl about the size of a large cereal bowl, with a bent handle attached to the top.

The cauldron is closely tied to the goddess, as it is symbolic of the womb—the vessel in which life begins. It also stands in for the element water, as filling a cauldron or any container is the best way to use water in any number of rituals. My cauldron lives just inside our front door in what has, over time, become an altar space for me.

An altar, while not something I ever set out to build, is something that in one form or another exists in many homes. It is a small space where I keep things precious to me, and if pressed, I could more than likely point out a few other sacred spaces spread across our cozy six-hundred-square-foot apartment. This one, however, is undeniably Wiccan-centric. It holds the vase Sam gave me, covered in the colors of autumn leaves and inscribed with our wedding date, that I fill with flowers every Samhain. Beside the vase stand two crystal candleholders, filled with a black and a white candle respectively, which we light every equinox. Around the vase rest the flower crowns the kids and I wear every Beltane, and my cauldron sits smack in front of it all.

My cauldron has never bubbled, alas. It really only serves one purpose, but it's one I value greatly. In it, at all times, are two bundles of dried sage. One is the bundle that was lit on our wedding day, to clear and honor the space in which we took our vows, and one is the bundle I use routinely in our home. The bundle from our wedding I try to use every year on our anniversary. I rarely let it burn long, as I have a crazy attachment to it. The other gets replaced on a pretty regular basis. Sage is used to "smudge" a space, or clear it of unwanted energies. You can use it to create a sacred space, like we did at our wedding, or you can simply use it as a method of cleaning, like I do in our home: I open our windows and light the smudge stick (as the bundle of sage is called), and slowly walk through our home, imagining the bad energy leaving and holding in my heart what I want our home to be filled with—love, joy, safety. When I'm done, I carefully rest the smudge sticks in my small iron cauldron, keeping them safe and ready to use when next I need them.

Some witches will use their cauldrons to scry by filling them with water, some to combine herbs and plants for ceremonial use. I imagine someone out there has simply put a plant in one. Either way, a metal bowl of any size is pretty handy to have about, and most witches will inevitably have one meeting some requisite need or occasion.

Since I'm on a roll, I might as well add a broom to the list, right? I mean, I'm a witch—it does feel like a necessity. Of course I own one.

Most witches' brooms are not the kind you can buy at Walgreens with an attached dustpan, obviously. (Though if we're going to be honest here, that one gets a lot more use in my house and at times is used with as much attention and intention.) The proper name for the broom as a magical tool is *besom*, and it is made of all-natural materials that are better for a good ceremonial cleaning than a clean sweep. The handle is usually of carved ash wood, the bristles of birch twigs bound with willow. The ash is aligned with masculinity and fire, the birch femininity and fertility, so the broom is a symbol of unification. They are used in handfasting ceremonies across many cultures, in which the bride and groom hold hands and "jump the broom" together.

The besom, however, isn't just for handfastings. This is where I'd kill to tell an amazing flying-broom story, but alas. However, the besom has a variety of uses, each of which is unique to the witch. Common practice will find witches hanging their broom by the front door, under the belief that it will protect the family within. It is also believed that a witch's broom has the power to sweep out harmful spirits from a space. Mine comes out on a somewhat regular basis, often along with the sage, to clear our space and push out any negative energy. When our children were small, I would sometimes sweep out the room in which they slept, wishing them only good dreams and peaceful slumber. Today, a small besom hangs near the door of my children's bedroom as a protective talisman.

I'd love to tell you I have a wand, but sadly, I can't. Wands serve the same role as the besom in a lot of ways, acting as a tool to direct energy. Athames, too, are used for this. Athames are knives with a black or dark handle that are specifically *not* used for cutting. They are dull and double-edged and purely ceremonial.

Bolines are the sharp knives witches set aside for special use, more often than not when needing to cut herbs or cords or inscribe a candle. Any knife will do, of course, but it is nice to have one dedicated to the purpose. Often, bolines will have a white handle and be shaped not unlike a crescent moon or a scythe. My habits around knives are a bit unconventional, as you are just as likely to see me using an ulu to chop the herbs as pulling out my pocketknife engraved with *Be Brave Be True* on the side to do just about anything else.

Really, the tools used in a given practice can be anything that has a particular meaning to the witch. The point is to always use the selected tool with intention. Having specific items for specific uses helps ground that intention but is by no means necessary. I have a wooden spoon I bought years ago that has the symbol of the goddess engraved on the bowl. It sits in my utensil crock, smooshed in with no ceremony whatsoever. Yet sometimes, when I am feeling I need the reminder, or just need an extra boost of intention for what I'm cooking, I will dig it out from amongst the various other large spoons and spatulas. I will feel the worn wood and run my finger over the symbols burned on it and feel just a bit more in the moment, a bit more intentional.

I suppose you could say the tools don't make the witch, the witch makes the tools, but that feels a tad bit hokey to me. Also, I have "made" none of my tools. That said, the bowl you treasure from your grandmother that is absolutely perfect to make cookies in? I'm pretty sure it's magic.

I PUT A SPELL ON YOU

THE TRUTH ABOUT
SPELLS AND CURSES

B Y THIS POINT YOU MAY BE WONDERING: IS THERE ANY ELEMENT OF magic in Wicca? Do *I* believe in magic? Spells? Is *any* of that true?

I admit that long before I was a practicing witch, I was a believer in magic. I'm a wishing-on-stars, intuition-following, penny-picking-up, fairy tale–loving kind of girl. I always have been. I have always reveled in the wonder of the world. It was framed differently in my youth, created by an omniscient God and fostered by saints, but it was there nonetheless. The mystical has always been something I adored and sought out. The idea of a fairy tale, a personal myth—the two were forever intertwined in my heart. Who doesn't love a happy ending?

It's just that I have come to understand, deep down, that happy endings are created from the inside out.

EVER AFTER

I do not believe a star can change your life, or that a spell can create a pumpkin carriage. I have never believed in cursed spindles or waking kisses. However, I do believe in the power of our intentions. I believe a wish can be the beginning of a great effort. I believe that every once in a while, the universe aligns just right and fairy tales have their chance. I believe in letting in the joy of this fact and delighting in the unknown. I try to be ready to recognize those moments when they happen. I believe, as Roald Dahl wrote, "Those who don't believe in magic will never find it."

I might not put much stock in magic wands or bibbidi-bobbidis, but there's so much in our world that defies explanation, so much we have yet to learn. Today, many of the things people once thought of as magic have been proven otherwise—but who is to say that just because something is real, because it can be categorized and explained, makes it any less magical? I say it can make it even more so. Every step toward understanding opens up worlds of unknown and miraculous new occurrences.

So, yes, I do believe in magic, but perhaps not the kind most people think of when they ask the question. I don't believe in rabbits out of hats, or that certain words and candles will bring you luck or money or love. I don't believe we can control the world around us any more than we could capture and hold the wind.

I believe the moment my son read a sign in our neighborhood on his own for the first time was magic. I believe the shower of magnolia blossoms in our garden every spring is magic. I believe the sound of my daughter laughing in her sleep is the best magic of all. I believe magic happens in the place where our own wonderment and the amazingly inexplicable intersect. I believe magic happens when we feel connected, at peace, and full of hope.

I believe, too, that we can *create* magic. We can change the world—or at least we can change our part in it. We can affect those around us, influence moments, and set courses. I believe in intention, and I think you will find most witches feel the same. Magic is not elusive, it is not confined to the pages of secret, locked books. It lies there within our hearts. It is within our power to create, to move, to transform.

We are divine, after all.

So how does this happen? This is where I give you a list of short rhymes and crazy ingredients, right? Where we plot the planets and light candles? Alas, no. Not that those practices don't have valid reasons for existing. But all those traditions, simply put, are ways for a witch to find his center, to bring himself into the moment. I don't use them, but that doesn't mean they aren't effective for some. Nothing can change, and our actions mean very little, unless we can undertake them with absolute intention.

More often than not, we live in between. We agonize over or long for the past, we speed toward the future. We are very rarely fully in the present. I am often simultaneously worrying about something that happened last week while planning next week's meals, completely missing what's happening right in front of my face. When I spend time agonizing over things I wish I could do over and trying to perfect the things I have yet to start, I completely miss the moments I have control over. Worse, I miss moments of true magic as they're happening. I miss my daughter's story of her day or my son's outstretched hand for a "fives." When we are lost in all the time that isn't, we can't act with true intention, because we are too busy reacting or predicting. We cannot create without being present, without focusing on what it is, in this moment, that is most needed.

So we light a candle. We say a small phrase. We lay out cards that can only tell us what we already know. We trace the lines across our palms and hold quartz against our chests. We create rituals that bring us back from the worries and anxiety and plans and forecasting. We create practices that pull us from wherever we are to the place we are meant to be. We can make the world stop spinning if we so choose; we need only to be present. We need only to find the ways to bring us back: the rituals that allow us to pause, to breathe, to live intentionally.

I twist the ring on my finger three times out of habit. I touch the evil-eye charm at my throat. I remind myself to take a breath and pause. Stop. I lower the volume on the voices in my heart, the ones telling me I'm failing or falling or not prepared. I breathe deep and feel the centuries of history resting below my feet, and I let them hold up my weight. I lift my spirit up to the sky, past the blue to the stars made of the same dust in my bones.

I try, if only for a short breath, to stand in my place—in time, in life, in the world—to stand in my own divine power and honor it. And like anything else, the more I do it, the easier it gets.

Right now is when we have the most power. Here, in this moment, is where you can create the grandest change.

Of course, once you are there, once you are settled and ready to put forth energy and power and creation into the world, what then? We all have a list of wants and worries, of things we wish could or would change, and if there is divine power within us, then why not? Why not create a spell for money or luck or even just health? According to pretty much every story ever written, all it should take is intense focus and the wave of a wand. What spells are, what that word has come to mean, has largely been defined by popular culture: a wave, a rhyme, a bubbling vat or a raging bonfire.

I don't believe it works that way. I believe the role of the witch isn't to recite an incantation to bring her whatever she or someone else asks for. I don't believe what we see as "spells" can do that. What I believe is that we create our own refuge. That we can, on occasion, reach into our shared consciousness and generate change. I believe we can create the energy needed to fill our space with what it is we truly need, if we can quiet ourselves enough to hear what that is.

CHARMED

After I had Samaire, I stayed home for seven months with her. The company I worked for was amazing and let me have the time, and my husband and I had saved madly for a long time previous to make it easier. I cherished those months. I still do. I rarely, if ever, put her down during that time. I would rock her and sing to her, and when the inside of our small apartment was too close, we would wander outside into the great city that enveloped us. I knew every crack in the sidewalk of our neighborhood. I knew each wrought-iron-gated stoop, and every Latina grandmother sitting on those stoops knew us. We took countless walks through Central Park as I showed her every small flower, every fallen leaf. We watched the ducks in the turtle pond and counted the squirrels along the Literary Walk. I quoted poems and plays to her from the authors looming over us as giant stone statues. I spent many an hour quietly singing her show tunes as we sat on the red bleachers beneath the blazing lights of Times Square.

Each day was perfect, and I felt absolutely whole. Then, one day—out of nowhere, it seemed—I could suddenly feel the days flying by and my deadline looming closer. I had to go back to work. I needed to. But I was going to have to leave her behind. To say it was a heartbreaking realization would be the largest understatement I can fathom. It was devastating. I fully recognized I had been given time most mothers were not, and I felt absolutely lucky for it—spoiled, actually—but the thought of someone else caring for my baby, someone else comforting her when she cried, someone else witnessing any of her firsts, no matter how small, was almost more than I could bear at the time. My heart hurts now just writing about it.

It was one of those times when I wanted the wand-waving, spell-casting, cauldron-bubbling version of witchyness to be real. I wanted to say some words and have the world turn exactly as I wished. I cried myself to sleep for nights on end and felt absolutely powerless. This wasn't what I wanted. It wasn't who I wanted to be.

However, I wasn't powerless, as much as it felt that way. I decided to create my own small spell to help Samaire, and myself, through what was bound to be a very trying day (week, year). After a ridiculous amount of searching, I found a locket that was just right. It fit in the palm of my hand and had a brass dragonfly emblazoned across its front. Dragonflies are symbols of transformation, of adaptability—they are born in the water, then rise into the air and fly. Dragonfly totems represent the idea of that adaptation: the ability to evolve, to take the next step. I knew in my heart that this next step was best for Samaire and me both in the long run. I just needed to allow myself to evolve, to trust and adapt, to make it happen. Dragonflies also have amazing flight patterns, easily changing direction as they glide through the air. Dragonflies remind us to be joyous in changing times, to remember through the change that we are still flying. I needed that reminder. I wanted to work. I was lucky enough to be able to work and I was lucky enough to have a safe place to bring my healthy, happy child. This situation was difficult, but it was also pretty wonderful. I needed to remember that.

I placed a photo of Samaire in the locket, opposite a photo of Sam with her. I needed to consider I wasn't the only one having to leave her behind. I wasn't alone; we were doing this together, for the betterment of our family. I then carefully picked out her softest onesie, blanket, and lovey and put them in our bed for the night, to make sure they would smell like home when she was somewhere new. I said a few words over all of them as I put them in her diaper bag the next morning. *Keep her safe. Keep her happy. Don't let her be afraid. Remind her I love her.*

It didn't make the leaving of her any easier. We both cried. However, I had faith the love I had imbued into those items would help her, and I held that locket in my hand or over my heart all day. It reminded me multiple times that change is scary, and sometimes it hurts, but it can be done. I did my best to find joy in it. I showed off photos of my beautiful girl while feeling the giant hole in my heart. I held the locket tightly and sent her all my love and comfort when a moment came where I felt she needed me. I breathed deeply and asked the wind to carry my words to her.

Every day for weeks I followed my small ritual. Into our bed went her onesie, blanket, and lovey. Over my heart went the locket, over her bag my words of hope. I kept myself in the moment. I strove to not worry about tomorrow or cry over what was to come. I held her when I had her. And every day it got a bit more bearable. It never got easier; she still carries a large piece of me with her when she walks in the other direction. I still miss her terribly, and a small ring (kept company by another for her brother) has replaced my locket, broken long ago from years of use, years of giving me comfort, years of being held too tightly in my hand. I miss my children, still, every day. I wonder if I will ever leave them and not feel as if I were leaving behind a limb, or a vital part of my heart. But it's a gift, the ability to send them to play and learn and be joyful without me. It's a gift that I can go do things I love until we reunite.

I didn't need a wand all those years ago when I most wanted one. I needed strength and support. I needed perspective and hope. I needed to remember what was important, to be reminded to live in the moment. I created my own magic in that locket and those small words uttered over a baby bag.

Spells are simply prayers sent inward to our hearts instead of outward to a separate being. I do not ask a god to give me answers or provide me comfort. I send my hopes and fears out into the greater world so that they may come back to me with a bit of clarity. I hold what's important to me in my heart and use my own power to make it happen. I focus my energy on what I can do, what words will give me comfort, and what deeds will best support positive outcomes. Then I take action. I claim responsibility for my reaction to what's happening and make it better. Or I don't. I live with the consequences either way.

We honor our own power and the power that surrounds us when we remember that we are but a small piece of a great, wondrous existence. Being a witch, for me, is providing hope and joy and comfort to those around me. It's about people more than wishes. What is more magical than being able to provide comfort to someone through a well-timed word or sympathetic smile? What is more empowering than finding a way through a difficult situation by seeking strength and consolation within your own being?

A Wish Your Heart Makes

Simple, small things mean something. I live my days striving to remain in the moment, to bring intention with every action, to pour forth good energy into the world and into every act I'm a part of. I don't succeed all the time, but I try.

Samaire and Wylie and I cook together. When we stir, we stir clockwise so that the food we make helps propel the people who consume it forward. We stir hearts in with the spoon, so that the ones eating our food will feel the love we put into it. When we are having a particularly hard morning, I kiss Wylie's hand and draw a small heart where my lips touched. He carries my love with him through the day then, knowing he is cherished. These are small things but they are our spells, our everyday acts done with great intention. They are ways to create love and care and tenderness to share and carry forward.

You do spells, too, I have no doubt. What is the lasagna recipe your grandmother used to make other than a spell? What is the song you sing as you rock your children to sleep, or the music you danced to at your wedding? What are these things but small acts of intention meant to bring nourishment, comfort, and love? The poem you read over and over, or the book that will never close properly because it's been so thoroughly devoured? The necklace you wear when you are homesick? These are spells, totems, and talismans—all ways we connect with something greater outside, or deep within, ourselves. Every day I have my own ways of connecting and nurturing my intentions, weekly and daily rituals that ground me and propel me forward. They are little things, almost tics that I sometimes repeat without thinking.

Sometimes, when life gets too much, when the kids are going crazy from being inside all day or my job has overflowed into my "real" life, leaving precious little breathing room, I forget about intent entirely. Life has a way of creeping in that way, of robbing us of the gift of living fully aware. Still, I go through the motions, and on my worst days simply the movement of the action can bring me back to where I need to be: present in the moment, where I can begin to act once again with intention.

Then, suddenly (or, more often than not, seepingly slowly) my actions take on meaning, and I remember this food I'm cooking will nourish my family, this rug I'm vacuuming will harbor my children's grand adventures. This home shelters them; it is their refuge, and so my everyday tasks take on new meaning. I think of the things that have haunted us all week—my short temper, my son's never-ending fight against bedtime, my husband's late-night work call, my daughter's never-ending homework. I take my broom and carefully think of all the moments when we weren't our best, all the energy that we let go of here in our home that was damaging and unkind. I reach into the corners of the room and my heart and I slowly sweep them out the door. I purposely choose to rid our home of our worst moments, sweeping them out into the greater world and away from our safe place. My broom may not fly, but it is magic nonetheless.

I think of what I want for us, what I want for our home, as I pick up the LEGOs from under the couch and the small pairs of underwear from the hallway. (How?! Why?! Is this just *my* house? I have to wonder.) As I rearrange the papers proudly displayed on our fridge, I thank all the world for this moment. I dust off our photos and think, *May we always be this happy.* I rearrange the little knickknacks on our shelf and hope the world always feels so small, so warm.

In essence, I live my life. I clean my house just like you do and I do my best to take parts of those tasks and make them a more conscious act, a small prayer. Is every chore a holy act? Hell, no. Do I think kind, hopeful thoughts while crouched over the toilet wiping away the evidence of my son's poor aim? I do not. Believe me when I say that if I held faith in curses, that is when they would be cast. A lot of cursing does happen, in fact. It's just the more familiar, secular kind; I'm not actually damning him in any way.

Mostly.

BIG WHEEL
KEEP ON TURNIN'

LIVING THE DAY-TO-DAY AS A WITCH

I OFTEN HAVE DAYS WHERE I FEEL COMPLETELY OVERWHELMED. I'LL walk to work and feel, with every step closer, the weight on my shoulders getting heavier. I worry about the people I work with, if I am doing my best by them; about my own responsibilities; about whether or not I am doing my very best for my career. I worry about all the normal things people worry about. The weight grows ever heavier.

I try to pause in those moments. I try to remember this *is* just a moment, and take the time to become present. As I walk, I attempt to feel more a part of what surrounds me. I remind myself that I walk a path that people have been walking for centuries. My feet are retracing their steps, and beneath the slabs of cement and steel on which I walk are miles of soil and stone. I am but a moment in time. I am paving the way for those coming behind, as those who went ahead did for me. I am not alone. Not really.

If the footstep of a dinosaur can survive millions of years, then something I do this day might change the world for the better. There is power in me—in all of us. We *are* the divine power; we are no lesser or greater than anyone else. The divine rests in every living thing, and so it should be honored. Each of us holds within us the creative power that set our world spinning. It is within us to live up to that power held in our hearts.

Wicca sets up that promise. If that divine energy lives in all living things, then it lives in each of us, and we are all connected. What can I do to fulfill that promise? What is in me that I can offer to the world? Instead of trying to live up to the rules of some unknown force, instead of acting through fear of consequence, Wicca offers me a chance to live up to my potential all on my own; it challenges me to do so. It opens the world in a way that didn't feel possible to me before.

I'm not a witch because I call myself one. Living as a witch is striving to live a kind and wise life without harm to others, never seeking power from the suffering of someone else or choosing personal benefit through the denial of another person. I am a witch because I live by those tenets. I'm a witch because I have divine power within me and I believe it resides in you as well. I'm a witch because I strive every day to understand my place on the great wheel of life and do my best while in that place to live up to the promise the power within me provides.

True change comes from not just recognizing our own power but finding ways to focus it. In Wicca, we have a universe of symbology and totems, stories and history, to draw from to focus our power and ourselves. There are stones and cards and runes and herbs. There are any number of practical items to draw us to a place where we can focus and appreciate where we are, to remind us of the power we have to continue, to overcome, to enlighten.

Some witches name the divine power they find in themselves, honor it by associating it with a god or goddess, or both, to whom they relate. They strive to have the wisdom of the Greek goddess Athena or create the homely warmth and love of the Norse Frigg and Freya. Some of us wear tokens with symbols on them to ground us, to remind us of what is important or what we are striving toward. Some build small altars in their home for the same purpose.

To honor a goddess, to seek in her image a reminder of what's possible, isn't necessarily synonymous with worship. Some witches do worship various goddesses, others simply feel the power of their stories and connect with them on a level that reminds them of their own power, that lends strength and hope when they might need it most. For me, this connection has often simply been about meeting the right goddess at the right time.

Years ago, when Sam and I were just short of our first wedding anniversary, we traveled to Ireland to see some dear friends get married themselves. We were only there a few days, but per our usual travel philosophy we packed as much as we could into that short time. (This is where I stop and share with you how Sam and our friend John were so excited to be in Ireland, home of the great Guinness, that they went for two whole days without eating a single meal leading up to dinner, as the foamy nectar seemed almost singularly able to sustain them. I, on the other hand, ended up desperately buying an egg salad sandwich from a train station vending machine on the second day and forcefully declaring that our days of living on beer alone were through.)

On our whirlwind excursion through Ireland, we hopped on a bus-and-train tour from Dublin to Galway, with various stops between. One of those stops was the Bunratty Castle and Folk Park, in County Clare. There I found everything I had hoped to see in Ireland, or at least the one thing I had hoped see: a cottage just like Sean Thornton's in *The Quiet Man*. I took dozens of photos of the modest white thatch-roofed home while Sam patiently waited for our walk through the castle.

I was less interested in the castle. In my mind, I thought it would be just a series of old stone rooms, but I went along in hopes that the view from the top of its walls would be beautiful. We got to the castle just in time for a tour, and before I knew it I was wandering along with a dozen other tourists listening to the grand history of—you guessed it—a bunch of stone rooms. (I am doing it, of course, a great disservice; the tour was informative and the castle fully furnished. I, however, was easily distracted and fully famished. The timing was off, for sure.)

We finally got to the last part of the tour, the Great Room, where our very friendly guide stopped to show us a small carving in the wall—from what I could tell, a rather lewd carving in the wall. I was suddenly interested.

Hand placed on her pregnant belly, the guide began to tell us the legend of Sheela-na-gig. She confirmed the carving was, in fact, a woman with hands placed on either side of her exposed vulva. She regaled us with the curious proliferation of similar carvings across Ireland and mainland Europe. No one knew for sure what it was, what it might mean, but there were theories. One that particularly rang true for her, as well as many of the other guides there at the castle: Sheela-na-gig was the earth goddess. She was a holy symbol of birth and life. It was said that if a woman was having trouble getting pregnant and honored Sheela-na-gig, the goddess would bless her with a pregnancy.

Our tour guide smiled and pointedly looked at her burgeoning stomach.

"I'm not the only guide in such a predicament. We all blame the Sheela."

She laughed and asked for questions, and then our small groups dispersed to further explore the castle.

I stayed in that room.

Sam wandered about, checking out the copious weaponry hanging on the walls, while I inched closer to the carving of the mysteriously proud yet somewhat obscene goddess.

The stone was rubbed smooth in places where people's fingers had touched it. I thought about all the women over time who had approached this strange little deity in hopes of creating some sort of change, in hopes of sparking some sort of ancient magic. I thought about all the conversations Sam and I had started and meandered our way through about having children; we weren't ready yet but had talked at length about what we'd like to have happen. I thought about the day when I was twenty years old and I was told by a doctor I likely wouldn't be able to have children, about how hard it had been to tell Sam that we might not have kids the way he might have always imagined. I thought about how miracles happen every day, how our journey down this path hadn't even started and yet already I carried this sliver of pain in my chest that hurt so much I couldn't put words to it.

I dreamed, for a moment, of children with Sam's bright blue eyes. I stood in that centuries-old castle in front of the earth goddess, who stood for the very promise of creation.

"Go ahead. You've nothing to lose."

Sam was right behind me. He knew everything that was running through my head. He knew I carried around that sliver of pain, that I had done so for years now and it had only gotten more painful once I found the heart I wanted to help fill.

I reached out and placed my two fingers gently on the smooth spot on the goddess's forehead, and I felt the legions of women who had done the same: women who had stood exactly where I was standing, reached out just as I was, touched where my fingers rested. These women, like me, were wishing and hoping to become a goddess of creation themselves. They looked at this small carved figure in a wall and perhaps thought they, too, had nothing to lose.

I thought of the sadness of the women who, over the centuries, had stood where I stood then—women who were desperate, living in societies where their ability to have a child was the measure of their worth. Or women who were heartbroken over one unsuccessful pregnancy after another, grasping for whatever hope they could find and looking into this strange goddess's eyes, believing she could help them.

I stood humbled.

My journey had not even begun; what lay before me was still unknown. The pain I carried in my chest was insignificant when I thought of the women who had come before me. The pain I felt in my heart was lessened with the thought of it being a shared burden. We had all come to this place: joyful with promise, desperate in yearning, searching for hope. The line of women I had now joined in this place was long and vast and infinite. The goddess had seen to them all. She had stared out of this small square of stone and promised them all that they held creation deep inside of them—of us.

My story doesn't end with me going home to find I was magically with child; Sam and I were still some time off from actively seeking to add to our small family. But it does end happily. That brief moment standing before Sheela-na-gig turned something in my heart, reminded me that hope isn't worth giving up when you still have yet to begin the journey. Sheela reminded me that I was one of a great line of women in this world who all dreamed of the same thing, and I had not only my own strength and fortitude to draw from but theirs as well.

That ache in my heart lessened just a bit.

Sheela is but one of the thousands of goddesses who appear across stories and myths from around the world. Out of all of those goddesses, Sheela-na-gig, that strange, mysterious goddess, had found me just when I needed her.

Being a witch, to me, isn't necessarily about using words to pull things out of thin air or waving wands to create change. Sometimes it's about being brave enough to say out loud your heart's deepest desire, so you can begin the work to make it happen—so you can make room in your heart and your life for the miracle you're hoping for. I hope, if anything, that's what you have gotten out of my long-winded explanations and rambling stories: that above all, being a witch is more about people and peace than incantations and pointed hats. It's magic, all right, but perhaps not the kind that appears in all our stories.

THESE ARE THE DAYS OF MIRACLE AND WONDER

R A I S I N G   M Y   C H I L D R E N
W I C C A N   (N O T   W I C K E D)

With all I've previously said about the magic I believe in, I should make clear that I do not believe magic is confined to appear *only* in small acts. I might not believe we can control the weather or change the tide with a simple whispering of words, but I do believe that words have tremendous power and that there are times when we can use them to create something lasting. I believe in our ability to create a spell that will live on long after the moment in which we cast it is over. There are moments in time that are gifted to us to do great kindness and show great love, to build a story of our own—or, in this case, help begin someone else's.

In Wiccan traditions, a child's name is seen as so important that the announcement of it is recognized with a ceremony to which friends and family are invited. The purpose of this rite is to officially introduce the child into the community. The ceremony itself is called a "saining" or a "Wiccaning."

The ritual of Wiccaning originated in the 1960s, as Wicca became a regular practice in North America. The ceremony itself is not unlike a baptism in traditional Christian rites, or the Jewish bris. It is simply a way for the child to be announced to the universe, a way for the baby to join his or her world. As with all Wiccan ceremonies, there are no hard-and-fast rules for conducting a Wiccaning. The timing is up to the parents and often chosen in correlation with a natural event, such as the closest new moon, solstice, or equinox. Ideally, it is held outside, close to nature, as a reminder that the wheel now has a new participant, the earth a new creature to behold.

The Wiccaning is where the parents swear an oath to the baby, promising to raise him or her to the best of their abilities with love and kindness, protection and respect. They also seek the assistance of those who surround them, placing the child under the guardianship of their friends and family, who will help assure the child's safety and honored place among the greater community. Sometimes god/dess parents are chosen (also called the "guide parents"), and they make a promise to help shepherd the child through the world as well.

This ceremony is also where the parents will announce the name of the child. Sometimes the child will have both a legal and a Wiccan name, the latter of which may change when the child comes of age and chooses a different one; sometimes the child will be given only one name. Regardless of the details, the parents use this ceremony to introduce the child by name to the universe. Announcing the name via this rite is meant to seal the child's place as an individual with his or her own divine power and to begin the child's tale in this world.

A name, of course, is not merely a word used to refer. It is the first true outward definition of who this child might be. It is the collection of sounds, the song, that will echo through space and time, holding within it the story of a life. Because names are seen as carrying such power, you will often meet Wiccans who have adopted new names, names that make them feel more connected to the greater power or that create a distance between who they once were and who they are now striving to be. Naming ceremonies, therefore, are not always restricted to the birth of a child; they can also act as a gateway to a new life. They can easily be part of a welcoming ceremony for a new member of a coven or someone just joining the practice. Regardless of when or why a saining/Wiccaning happens, names are sacred in Wicca and are treated with the utmost consideration.

Sam and I chose not to have a saining for our children. Many of our friends and family live far away, and as I am a solitary practitioner, it made more sense for us to quietly create our own tradition around choosing their names and announcing them to those we love. I have always kept my traditions and practices very close, and especially with our children's names it felt right that whatever ceremony (or lack thereof) would exist should be something Sam and I did together, within our own small circle of rites as a newly formed family.

Despite the lack of formal ceremony, we did not take the responsibility of naming our children lightly. We still wanted our children to be able to live their own myths, to say their names and feel their own power. I wanted them to grow up knowing where their stories began and to feel what we had hoped for them, even when we are gone. I wanted us to give them something that would be worthy of the beginning of their story. Naming my children was the most powerful spell I would ever weave, the most hopeful prayer I would ever send into the universe—my first true gift to them. Words have power, intention has lasting effects, and names, in many ways, can define you.

Sam and I first talked about what we'd name our children on a road trip through Arizona. We were far from actually having the children—we were still dating, across a distance of a thousand miles at that. Yet, on a long, rambling highway through Oak Creek Canyon one day, we found ourselves waxing poetic about what we might name our kids. We compared family names; we told stories about people we had loved whom the other would never get to meet and about those we wanted them to spend time with someday. We shared the stories of our own names and discussed where they came from and if we would change them if we could. At the end, we had a list of maybes for baby names, despite the bigger maybe looming over all of it.

Four years later, as we stared down at the small white stick declaring us parents, that original conversation seemed very far away. The pressure seemed insurmountable—how could we ever find a name worthy of this small being we were bringing into the world? My list of needs was absurdly long. I wanted to give her the world in her name. It would be a prayer every time it passed my lips. It was a spell I would cast that would last long after I was gone. It needed to be perfect. It needed to hold love and hope. It needed to give her strength, to keep her safe.

This child's name had to be beautiful, strong. It needed to be different and have meaning—not just a good definition but meaning beyond its translation, something that connected her through time to who Sam and I were at this moment. I also knew we wouldn't be in New York forever, so I wanted to find a way to tie a piece of it to her, to find a name that imparted some of its strength, helping her have roots here.

I devoured websites filled with names and paged endlessly through book after book. I sent Sam link after link and list after list, but nothing ever felt right. And then, it seemed, her name came to us. I was paging through a magazine one day and there it was: Samaire ("Suh-*meer*-ah"). The woman in the interview whose name it was mentioned that her parents had discovered the name while vacationing in Ireland. It was Gaelic, she said, meaning "morning star." Sam and I both immediately loved it. Our wedding rings are inscribed in Gaelic, and it felt fitting our daughter would have a Gaelic name as well. The definition seemed meant to be: she would be our new beginning in so many ways, our shining light. The fact that she would share part of her name with her father was a wonderful bonus. It was perfect.

The elation didn't last long. It soon turned out that the name might not mean what we thought it meant. We discovered that Samaire might not be Gaelic at all; our friends who spoke Gaelic had never heard of the name. Its roots in Ireland were highly questionable. Was it possibly Irish? Perhaps, but increasingly it was seeming highly unlikely this particular epithet was what we had presumed. However, we had already fallen in love with it, so we hit the books. It had to mean *something*. A good bout of searching and a few trips down Internet rabbit holes led us to a site where the name's meaning was given as "elm tree."

The deal was done. I couldn't imagine a better moniker for our girl. Elm trees have always been special to me; they are closely aligned in myth and meaning with the goddess and are revered for their strength and resistance to splitting. They are seen as sentinels of the forest and symbolize hope in the Druidic practice. The elm tree had always been a natural totem I had felt particular kinship with, and it seemed fitting to connect my daughter to the greatness of the world around her by connecting her to the elm.

The elm tree was also precious to Sam and I personally. We live in a vast, remarkable city; it was our first home together and would be our daughter's first home, too. And while the skyscrapers and theaters and cacophony of people were amazing, our hearts found their home above all within the confines of Central Park. We would escape there on the weekends, eager to get to that perfect spot where you couldn't see the buildings or hear the cars. We got lost in the Ramble, watching robins in the spring and trudging through a million orange and red leaves in the fall. One of those falls, Sam asked me to marry him as the moon shone above us at Tavern on the Green. Central Park was magic.

Above all, however, our favorite place in that great park of parks was the Literary Walk. It consists of a wide sidewalk bordered on each side by giant stone statues of famous literary figures and is crowned by the large

American elms that create a canopy over it. These trees stand sentinel over the path and are absolutely beautiful regardless of season. Beauty, however, is not what makes this place or these trees extraordinary. What makes this place, this hallowed hall of nature, extraordinary is that this is one of the largest and last remaining stands of American elm trees in North America. Here amongst the steel and stone, alongside great authors and poets, stand trees that if grown anywhere else would very likely have been long gone. An infestation that began in the 1930s destroyed most American elms, but here, entrapped in the city, these trees still stand. Guarded by the great Hudson River, enclosed by steel buildings, and encircled by interminable lines of cars, they avoided the plague of disease that slowly killed their brethren.

I love the symbology of that. Here, in the middle of one of the world's greatest cities, is a beautiful, awe-striking stand of trees in deft partnership with the steel that rises alongside them. Those trees have saved my soul on days when I longed for clear skies and a clean wind. They save many of us in this city who need the reminder that there is still nature, still life, still wonder around us—and we, in turn, save them. Here on our tiny little island, crushed with people and smoke and smog, we provide them a physical shelter just as they provide us a spiritual one. Central Park would not be half so wondrous if it were not here in the midst of skyscrapers, and this city could not survive without this vast expanse of trees. They are at once wholly independent and completely intertwined.

Just like us: our small, precious family.

I find hope in this dichotomy, and it's something I want Samaire to remember her whole life through. Sometimes things that seem to have nothing to do with each other—worlds that don't seem to belong—can save each other in ways no one would ever expect. It's okay to be contrary to what the world around you expects; it might just be exactly what the world needs. Grow tall, grow strong, grow where you feel most at home. Define your own place and make it work, dig deep roots and reach straight up to the sky. You may be surrounded by figures completely opposite what you are or how you see yourself; they may end up being your redeemers. You will inevitably redeem them, too.

Our son's name was much the same. He needed his tale, his own myth to carry forth. It was simply a matter of finding the right one. This time, though, the perfect spell for his name seemed predestined. We had conviction from the beginning around what his name would be; we knew just to whom and what we wanted him tied. Where Samaire's name grew from the present, Wylie's had its roots in the past.

He was Wylie William from the very start. Before the doctors could tell us for sure he was a boy, I was buying small silver tokens with his name engraved on them. I knew, we knew, he was our Wylie from the moment we knew he was on his way.

The meaning of his name was also much easier to ascertain than Samaire's. We had a plethora of choices, all of which seemed perfectly descriptive. Depending on whether you chose the English or Anglo-Saxon or German roots, you got a new meaning: enchanted, determined, a resolute protector. It was a strong name with a certain warmth to it. It reminded me of persistent coyotes and wide-open spaces. Whereas Samaire's name gave her a piece of the place where we built our first home, Wylie's lent him a piece of the place we had come from, roots in the land and space where both Sam and I had grown up.

Wylie William spoke of endless horizons and storms that curled over the edge of the world and ran at you—a gray wall of omniscient clouds. It was wind that traveled over hundreds of miles from the mountains to reach you on the plains; it was infinite skies and innumerable stars. I wanted our son to have that spirit, to know what it was to feel boundless. I wanted him to never let anything dampen his power or his essence, to always be as big as he needed to be, to fill the horizons of his life. I grew up in Kansas, and Sam's family came from there. The state motto is *Ad astra per aspera*, "To the stars through difficulty." I wanted our son to carry with him that feeling that he could reach the stars no matter what lay before him. Important as well, they were the middle names of his great-grandfathers.

Faris Wylie Bell (Papa, to me) was not a perfect person; he was often gruff and not overtly warm. He was not the kind of grandfather who picked you up to toss you in the air, or the kind who would play tea party with you amongst dolls and worn stuffed animals. And yet he was mine, and I adored him. He adored me, in turn, in his own way. He would pretend not to know how to get to the stores in my hometown when visiting so that I would ride with him in the car. He would let me sit on his lap while we watched *The A-Team* and tell me how the show would end not long after the opening credits so I wouldn't get scared. He would buy me extra donuts. He snuck me sips of his Pepsi. He would sit on the wooden swing on his porch and pat the seat next to him. I'd curl up beside him and we'd swing in companionable silence. I grew up knowing there would always be a seat beside him just for me.

William was a bit of a tradition in the Stiers family, Sam's father's middle name as well as his grandfather's. Where Papa was fairly stoic and a bit distant in his quiet, steady love, Ted William Stiers could not have been more warm and hospitable. From the moment I first met him, he hugged me fiercely and treated me like family. He was unerringly kind and amazingly generous. He loved to laugh and was constantly sharing (somewhat inappropriate) jokes. He was my key source for all stories involving Sam or his dad as children. Over the years, I spent hours listening to his stories and laughing with him, and I never tired of it. He had a way of telling his stories that made me feel I had been there and that I belonged. His heart had room for me in his stories, room for me in his family. I feel absolutely blessed three times over that I got to meet him. Wylie William will have these men with him as he grows: their determination and will to survive, their strength and love. He will be able to sit with the silence as much as revel in his life and tell wonderful tales. My little Wyl' Bill will continue their stories, will walk in the footsteps of great men and carry on their names.

A name is, truthfully, just a bunch of letters strung together to form a moniker. It doesn't have to be filled with thought and meaning, and yet here we are: letters pulled from history and language, from long-standing stories and old friends, from family greatly missed or even of whom the details are long forgotten. Names have incredible power—not for the stories they come from or the research it took to define them but for the intention with which they are given, the love from which they derive. Like any action we take, they can be made into something more, something great, something powerful—they can become our enchantments, our invocations to the universe, if only we're willing to make them so.

Thinking of Wicca, and the life I live within it, as a journey to seek peace rather than answers has become central to my practice. I have learned over the years to accept and even savor no longer having all the answers to how we all came to be, whether there is some grand plan, and, if so, what it might be. I live my life the best way I know how, and it has always seemed the right paths come to me when I need them most. I have made peace with the fact that some questions will forever go unanswered.

At least I *had* made peace with that, until one day I found myself looking into astounding blue eyes that mirrored my own and uttering the dreaded words: "I don't know."

When I had children, it felt suddenly as if not only would my heart burst from the sheer love I felt for them, but my back might break from the weight that had just been placed on it. I had never known such hefty responsibility, and as my children grew, instead of lessening, the weight seemed to multiply. I was overcome with the constant need to protect them from all harm and provide them with everything they could ever possibly need: love, shelter, nourishment—and answers.

In many ways, I had built my adult life to this point on uncertainty, on finding answers as they came to me. I didn't have many hard-and-fast beliefs, and I had experienced both moments of profound insight and moments when I simply walked away realizing the world is indeed vast and often unknowable. I was okay with both. I just wasn't sure how to pass on that same outlook to the two inquisitive creatures who had recently invaded my home.

They had so many questions. I marveled at their capacity for wonder and curiosity, the way their minds instinctively tore things apart. How they could look at something from every angle and yearn to understand every inch of it. I reveled in their questions, and I promised myself I would strive to answer every one. *Why is the sky blue? What happens to worms in winter? Why is the moon sometimes out during the day and sometimes not?* Google and I became incredibly well acquainted.

Those were just the academic questions. There were also some queries that were more personal, and easier to answer: *What was your favorite book when you were my age? When did you learn to read? Did you draw when you were little? Why do you dye your hair?* These questions were absolutely amazing to answer, because I found one would lead to another, then another, and soon we would all be filing in the blanks. I could turn the questions back on them, and I got to see how they saw me, how they saw their world, what they thought of it, what their own small life philosophies were. It was *marvelous*.

Sam and I made a pact early on that we would answer every question our children asked us as accurately and honestly as possible. We vowed we would not push off answers because we didn't know, nor simply because we were tired. The latter stipulation proved truly trying—there were days I wanted desperately to yell*"Because!!!"* to that fifteenth round of "Why?" But overall, we kept our promise. Out would come Google, a scrapbook would be pulled off the shelf. I would promise one more answer.

But I couldn't answer all their questions. As much as I wanted to, some answers I just couldn't give in good conscience. Some questions had no one single answer—there was only what I thought, what others supposed. When we got around to those, it felt like I was absolutely failing them. I was their mama; I was supposed to be able to answer their questions, allay their fears, and explain the unknown. Suddenly, my own spiritual comfort with ambiguity was an unbelievable burden. What had felt empowering and liberating was now crushing and confining. I missed the ease of my youth, a time when the answer, whenever I was in doubt, was "Because God made it that way." I was floundering. I felt as if I were inadequate, making a hash of the one job of motherhood that meant the most to my children. I vacillated between wanting to let them find their own answers in time and feeling obligated to always be someone they could come to for the solidity of answers.

It took me a long time to realize my point of view was skewed: I had mistakenly categorized answers as *truth*. In the rush of wanting to be the very best mom I could, the mother Samaire and Wylie deserved, I had lost perspective on something vital: they needed guidance, not resolution. At the time, however, I couldn't see past what I thought were my own failings.

So the spiral began. Like mothers everywhere, I hopped aboard the guilt train; no matter what tactic I employed, I felt I had done them wrong. I wanted to give them the world *and* a soft place to land. Instead, I felt I was confusing them more than anything, because my answers didn't always match the world they lived in.

I had grown up surrounded by people ready to give me answers. When I was small, I knew that I was fearfully and wonderfully made. I knew what the rules were; I even had a charm bracelet to wear on my wrist to remind me of the top ten. I had a community of people who stood at the ready, filled with answers about how the world was made and why. I had shelves of books recounting the stories of the saints to guide me and books of prayers for when I had requests. There was a ceremony, a process, and a story for everything. It was all very safe. Everything was secure. I need not wonder, I need not fret.

I looked at my children, my small precious miracles of the universe, and wondered how I could possibly give that to them. The honest answer was, of course, that sometimes I wasn't going to be able to.

It had been a normal weekend and a quiet evening. We were watching one last show before bed, and I was picking up the sundries of our daytime adventures before we called it a night. I leaned down to scratch our cat, Schiele, behind the ears and realized something seemed off about her. Samaire called to her from the couch, and Schiele, struggling, slowly got up to head toward her.

Something wasn't right.

Schiele was a fluffy black cat I had gotten years ago, in another life, when I lived in a house with a yard and had ample space for pets. I had had another cat before her, Mucha, a golden Bengal. Mucha was very much my familiar. (*Familiar* is a term from Old European folklore. It was believed that a familiar was a spirit or animal guide who assisted the witch in her magic; they were sometimes said to have a small piece of the witch's soul inside them.) She had very little interest in anyone else until Sam came around, and then his lap became her favorite place, but even with that change it was clear to whom she belonged.

At that time, I lived close to very good family friends and I babysat their toddler, Sarah, on a regular basis. Sarah spent many a weekend trying to lure Mucha out to play, and Mucha would have none of it. She stoically stayed out of reach until Sarah had gone. Sarah couldn't have her own cat at home, and I decided Mucha needed some company. It seemed the perfect solution to get a kitten Sarah could actually play with when she stayed with me who would also provide Mucha some companionship.

Schiele was feral when I got her, rescued from a box on the side of a highway. She was all skin and bones and loud mews, but after some patient cuddling and careful feeding we got her healthy. Mucha immediately made it clear I was hers, and Schiele was relegated to second-class standing. She didn't lack for attention, however. Sarah still came over on a regular basis, and soon Schiele was cuddled and loved within an inch of her life.

Years later, when we had the kids, Schiele once again regained her position of cuddle monster. She never left the children's side, coming to find them whenever we returned home and sleeping with them every night. She was undeniably now *their* cat. They poked and grabbed and held on to her as babies. They picked her up and carried her across the apartment as soon as they started walking steadily, arms wrapped around her front legs, her back legs swinging. They wrapped her in blankets while playing house. She never faltered. She never hissed, she never complained. The love they had for her was palpable. I have absolutely no doubt it was returned in kind. So when she seemed a little off, Sam and I decided to take her to the vet as soon as we could to make sure she was okay. We agreed I would call the next morning, and then one of us would take her in to be checked out sometime in the coming days.

The next morning, she was right where we had left her in the living room. It was the first night I remembered her not sleeping in the kids' room. A little piece of me started to panic. Sam and I exchanged worried glances while Samaire and Wylie ate their breakfast and got ready for school.

"Be sure to give Schiele hugs!" we urged them. When they went to get their backpacks, Schiele slowly got up to see them off as usual, but with noticeably less vigor.

When I got to work, the first thing I did was call our neighborhood vet, whose hours on Google were stated to be ten a.m. to five thirty p.m. I soon found it wasn't quite that simple. Apparently, the vet took an oddly long lunch break and sometimes came in a bit later in the morning. He also sometimes left at four p.m. I begged for some of his elusively precious time in the morning, then in the afternoon, then the next day. I explained that it was something of an emergency. I was near tears, and my voice must have been rife with tension, because my boss, David, who is possibly the nicest boss and mentor a person could have, leaned back from his desk to look at me.

"Go now. I'll cover for you. We don't have any meetings this morning you can't miss. Take care of your cat."

You guys. Seriously. He was letting me leave work *for my cat.* I promised myself then and there I would pay that shit forward someday.

I blubbered my thanks all over the place as I quickly grabbed my stuff and ran to the door while dialing the vet's office to tell them that I would be coming with my cat and that I would wait until she could be seen. I probably sounded insane, because the poor nurse, who had seemingly been slammed just minutes before, said, "We'll be ready for you when you get here, sweetie."

The twenty-minute walk home from my office had never seemed longer. I cursed my inability to run it and constantly compared the time it might take in a cab against my pace. I was suddenly overcome with the realization that Schiele might be *really* sick—that she was, in fact, an old cat. She had been with me so long, it had never occurred to me there would have to come a day when she wouldn't be.

She had been with me through my first jobs, when I rode the tide of the dot-com bubble with a new role in a new company every nine months or so. She had been with me in my three-bedroom house; she had moved with me to New York City, into a tiny studio apartment. She had seen me through moving in with Sam, through a wedding and two pregnancies, and provided comfort when Mucha had died. She was Samaire and Wylie's oldest and best friend. I sped as fast as I could across midtown, feeling like I was on some sort of heroic mission. I would get her help! She would get better!

I raced, breathless, up the four flights of stairs to our apartment. (Sam swore to me when we moved in, fifteen years ago, that those stairs would get easier with practice. It was the biggest and most blatant lie he has ever told me.) I opened the door and Schiele stood to greet me . . . and collapsed.

Oh god. No.

I had to get her to the vet. I looked around for something to carry her in. We had a cat carrier, but she hated it, and I hated it, too, as it was the carrier we had taken Mucha to the vet in when she got sick and died. I didn't want Schiele to smell it and be scared. I rummaged through my closet and found an old diaper bag I had used up until recently to lug the kids' stuff around. I reasoned it would smell of them, or at the very least like their stuff, and there was probably nothing more comforting to Schiele than that.

I scooped my limp little cat into the bag, lined with a few old baby blankets I had found, and headed out. She didn't make a sound. Usually when she was outside, she told us all about it. Usually her head would stick out of her carrier, and she couldn't smell everything enough. This time, she was horribly still and silent.

I stopped a block from the vet and put my hand on her back. I was convinced she had already passed away. The tears started really flowing then. I clutched the bag to my chest that last half a block, knowing that if I hadn't already lost her, I probably would soon. My heart started to crack.

The vet, despite his unconventional business hours, was unbelievably kind. The nurses all shared sympathetic looks as the doctor left the examining room after seeing me. One quietly walked over and shut the door. They all knew I had a decision to make.

Schiele hadn't slipped away on our walk over, but she was very close. Her small body was shutting down. The vet patiently gave me all the options and then reminded me she had lived a long, full life. He had seen her just a month earlier, and she had been in perfect health then. This was sudden, and there was nothing I could have done.

I texted Sam as I laid my head next to Schiele's. The paper on the exam table crinkled by my ear, and I left a small wet spot from crying. I gave her pets and thanked her for staying with me this long. I held her close, like a baby, just as she had always loved. I promised her I would take care of her babies. I reminded her of how much they loved her and apologized that she didn't get to say good-bye to them. I wrestled with the thought of delaying it all until they were out of school, but I didn't want to make her suffer. I said good-bye.

The vet came back and gave her the shot that would put her slowly to sleep and take her away from me. He offered a long, rambling monologue (and you know I know rambling) about how this was the best way to die; it was peaceful and pain free. He knew a doctor, another vet apparently, whose assistant of decades was diagnosed with cancer. In the end, she was in the hospital suffering greatly and begged him to help her go with dignity. The doctor snuck in with this medicine and injected it into her IV and she quietly passed away.

In my grief-stricken stupor, it occurred to me he was telling me the story of one of his friends committing what amounted to murder in the state of New York.

"Well, it all turned out. He lost his license, of course. We'll take care of Schiele; the nurses have some papers for you to sign." I was ushered out.

I returned to work, where complete strangers handed me tissues throughout the rest of the day, and then I left early to clean our apartment before I picked up Samaire from school. Sam was getting Wylie from daycare.

We were going to have to tell them their pet had died.

As a mother, I knew logically that moments like this would happen. There would be occasions that would mark a "before" and "after" in their lives, and those moments would change them. I just hadn't realized I would be so utterly and specifically aware of any of them when they happened. As I walked to Samaire's school, I was conscious of every detail of the weather, the cracks in the sidewalk, the signs in the windows. What would she remember? What odd, minuscule aspect of this walk would stick with her for years, always reminding her of this day? Suddenly my grief over Schiele seemed unimportant. I was about to break my daughter's heart for the first time.

I picked her up from class, and we started to walk home. I debated when to tell her and soon found I wasn't sure I could wait until we were safely at home to break the news. Every step I took with her felt like a lie. A block from our street, she solved the dilemma for me.

"Did you take Schiele to the vet? Did they give her medicine?"

I took a deep breath and began my story. As my daughter began to sob, I held her hand tightly and told her how peaceful it was, how necessary. I told her all about how I wrapped Schiele up in blankets that smelled of her and Wylie.

I watched my little girl shatter before me and I shattered with her.

We got up those damned steps somehow, and I held her close as we sat on the couch. I squeezed her so tight she complained of not being able to breathe. She laid her head on my chest and brought her knees to her chin, and she suddenly fit as perfectly against me as she had when she was a baby. I was at a loss for words, and I heard myself repeating the same platitudes the vet had said to me: she lived a long life; she was well loved; she knew that.

Then the door opened, and Sam walked in with Wylie, who was openly and unabashedly sobbing and crying out Schiele's name. I opened my arms, Samaire made room for Wylie, and Sam wrapped his arms around all of us.

We four sat there on the couch, curled and wrapped up together crying for a very long time.

Sam and I watched as our children discovered what the death of a loved one felt like. It was torture.

Every cell in my being wanted to take this agony away from them; every ounce of me wanted to lessen this pain. My heart ached with the feeling of my utter uselessness. The words stuck on my tongue. My brain returned to its long-engrained habit of clinging to answers: I could tell them she wasn't really gone. I could tell them she was in a wonderful place. We could talk all about cat heaven and the happiness she would find there . . .

I looked at Sam and I could tell he knew exactly what I was thinking.

"I want to so bad," I whispered.

"I know."

But I couldn't. I wouldn't. I wouldn't tell them a story just to ease their pain if I didn't believe it. We sat that evening, all piled on the couch together, and talked about what Sam and I believe happens when you die. We stressed how important it is to love those around you while you have them, how even when they're gone, you carry the love they had for you in your heart.

We stumbled through. That night we tucked two very sad, very tired little creatures into their beds. The room felt like there was a tangible hole in it, and we all just curled around it. I kissed their foreheads and prayed they would dream of happy adventures with their furry black guardian.

We got through the following weeks and months with only occasional tears. We had multiple talks about death and shared many stories of not just Schiele but other loved ones who had passed, whom the kids had not gotten to meet or were too young to remember. It seemed to give them comfort. I learned a valuable lesson: choosing to live what I believed and offering guidance, not answers, to Samaire and Wylie was the best thing I could do. I could do no more than point them in a safe direction; they would eventually have to find their own way, their own answers, and their own truths.

Samaire and Wylie were coming up on a phenomenal age where we could have discussions about colossally complex topics and they were able to understand them and develop their own points of view. It felt like the perfect time to start talking to them about not just what we believed but what the rest of the world held dear. We had always tried to weave in other religious points of view to our family life, but our teaching on these points was mostly circumstantial: questions around dreidel-shaped chocolates or Easter egg baskets in the grocery store, the occasional Bible story reference. There was nothing that was purposeful and planned.

Ironically, despite the fact I've spent so much of my time defining my beliefs, before they joined us, I had never given much thought as to how Sam and I would raise our kids, religion-wise. In our time together, he and I had fallen into a rhythm of ceremony and celebration, following the wheel of the year and my Wiccan practice. It was never a big discussion. We knew what we held sacred and honored it. After we had our children, suddenly our choices carried more weight. Family asked if we'd baptize them, what our plans were.

Our plans were, and still are, very open. We answered family queries as best we could and made it clear our children would be raised as we lived. We weren't going to change our favorite restaurants or our travel schedules because we had kids, why would we change our spiritual practices? We have shared holidays from time to time, and while we've never celebrated a proper pagan holiday with either of our families, if we made it clear it was important to us to do so, I'm sure they would do their best.

So though we never really went into parenthood with a solid spiritual plan, we discovered that answering those curious questions of our family and friends started our own conversations that simply brought us full circle, to the place where we already were. It was important to us our children have a foundation of faith—not with an all-knowing god, but within themselves. It was vital to us they felt they had a place in and a responsibility to care for the world they inhabited—that they felt connected to something greater and they felt greatness within themselves.

So we are raising them Wiccan. As they get older, that takes on greater meaning. There are more questions to answer, more reasons to give. Never, however, are the reasons *Because this is the right way to believe, the right way to live or see our world.* It's just, *This is Mommy's way. Daddy believes in similar things, but not exactly the same things. That's okay, because you believe what's true to your heart. This is just where we're starting.* And because we aren't teaching them this is the only way, we try to also teach them about the other paths of belief. We don't frame anything as right or wrong. We also don't frame it as ultimate truth.

Once, on a road trip through the mountains of Colorado, Sam's mom asked if she could get the children a Bible. I was pregnant with Wylie at the time, and Samaire had just turned three. I paused in my answer. I had never considered the question before. Sam and I had just begun to navigate how and what and when to teach the kids about religion, and I admit I wasn't sure I was quite ready yet to introduce them to the place I had so thoroughly left behind. Yet I immediately felt guilty. Here she was, offering to share her faith with the kids in a very innocuous way, and I was struggling to accept it. I should have been able to jump at the *Of course!* but instead I sat there, my heart larger than it should have been in my chest, as we wove around the mountain.

Happily, Sam made up for my internal struggle by answering right away: "Sure. We'll read it to them like we would any other storybook."

Yes. A part of me settled at that. It felt right: We would teach them the stories. They could decide for themselves which meant the most to them, which rang true. And so that's what we have done.

The books, the holidays, the ceremonies of different faiths are all ways for people to learn how to live their best lives, to answer questions that evade easy answers. We stress that every person, every group of people, has their own stories just as we have ours. And that's what they all are: stories. We explain that narratives, fables, and allegories help people understand and act out what it means to be the very best kind of person they can be.

We try to stress to them the commonalities more than the differences. Every spring, when the windows of our avenues are overcome with baskets and eggs and jelly beans and the bodegas bursting with lilies, I explain how just as we are celebrating the joy that comes with the return of the buds on the trees and birds in their nests, Christians are celebrating the resurrection of their savior. Is it any wonder, as the earth wakes after a long cold winter, we would all be celebrating a return to life?

Our stories may differ, the divine power may shift in where it rests— but in our hearts we have more in common than it may seem.

The summer after Schiele died, we were planning a trip through Istanbul and Greece. It seemed the perfect opportunity to introduce the kids to different religious viewpoints in a more in-depth way. We would be lucky enough to be in Istanbul during Ramadan, an amazing chance to talk to the kids about Islam. Our trip to Greece would run through Santorini, Crete, and Athens, so we stocked up on mythology texts.

We spent the months beforehand reading tale after tale of the Greek gods. We bought books on the contributions Islamic culture has made to the world and books on Ramadan and what it was about. The kids ate them up. We showed them on maps where the stories told in their books took place, where Athena faced off with Zeus or the Minotaur roamed his labyrinth. We showed them where we would be as we traveled through the stories we were telling. It added a whole new level of anticipation to our vacation. We couldn't wait to see in person all the places we had read about. I knew that a lot of what we read and talked about might be a little over their heads. I wasn't sure they totally understood the religious aspects of it all, but their excitement over the stories alone was worth all our studying.

Our first stop was Istanbul. This is where I have to pause for a moment and say if you ever get a chance to go to Istanbul, do it. Heck, do it now. It is the most beautiful, awe-inspiring city I have ever set foot in. We were fully aware when planning our trip that Turkey was rife with political conflict, and many of our friends and family tried to deter us from going, but it is absolutely the most wonderful city we have ever been to. We arrived at the Hippodrome just as families were collecting in the open spaces to break their fast. The kids ran across the lawn in front of the Hagia Sophia, playing tag among all the other children. Sam and I stood alongside the other parents watching over their broods. All felt right with the world as the final call to prayer resounded as if from the very sky itself, and everywhere around us a cacophony of joy broke out as families shared their meals. That night, we took Samaire and Wylie to see the Whirling Dervishes and explained the different cultures we were lucky to be witnessing. We discussed why Muslims fasted during Ramadan and for how long; we talked about how we, too, had traditions to remind us of what was important.

We spent the next few days wandering the beautiful, winding streets of Istanbul, the calls to prayer ringing above our heads throughout the day in an otherworldly fashion. Everyone we met treated the children and us kindly, pinching Wylie's cheeks and stroking Samaire's hair as though they were rare treasures. On our last day, we delved into the heart of Sultanahmet, the Old City of Istanbul. There, the Blue Mosque stands elegantly at one end of a large mall that is capped at the other end by the breathtaking Hagia Sophia. Sophia at one time was the largest cathedral in the world, then a mosque, and now a secular museum. It is an incredible thing, to stand there between them. You can't not be touched by the sheer history of centuries of sacred space.

I had spent a good portion of our morning making Samaire and Wylie swear they would be on their absolute best behavior when we entered the Blue Mosque that afternoon. Wylie knew to take off his shoes, and Samaire and I had worn long skirts; I put on a headscarf. We stressed over and over that it was imperative we show respect; we were entering someone else's hallowed hall.

I don't know what I expected, but I was breathless as we walked through the arches into the main space. The cathedrals of my youth had often been dark places, filled with overwhelming architecture. They were beautiful, yet weighty; they had always made me feel small. Whereas this? This space was fundamentally different. This whole room seemed to soar and take me with it. It was bright and filled with light. The whole space was filled with the blue of the tiles and the light streaming through the many stained-glass windows. The walls were elaborately decorated with calligraphic phrases. We couldn't read them, but they were, nonetheless, meaningful.

My threats and cajoling of the morning proved unnecessary; the kids were as speechless as Sam and I were. We walked slowly across the mosque, taking a moment to kneel and appreciate the sheer gravity of where we were. Samaire asked if it was wrong that her favorite part was the flooring (supremely cushioned for kneeling). Wylie counted the chandeliers. I adeptly avoided answering a question about why the women had to pray off to the side.

We left the mosque somewhat reluctantly and stepped out into the bright, steamy afternoon. However, we didn't leave any of the magic behind. Around the corner from the steps we were on was a beautiful walled-in plaza called the forecourt. Along its walls were giant panels referencing the history of Islam and, in turn, the Abrahamic religions.

I stood for a second in awe and then grabbed Samaire's hand.

"Come with me. This is important."

We walked, together, around every inch of that plaza and read every giant poster. I tried to point out bits of stories she might find recognizable, tried to point out places where phrases or holidays intersected with things that would be familiar to her. We finally stopped in front of the last board. It towered in front of us. Wylie came over with Sam, and I explained what it was.

"This is a family tree. You know, like the ones you made in school, or the one Mommy's working on that shows our family history—how Mommy and Daddy are connected to their mommies and daddies and they are connected to *their* mommies and daddies, over and over, back and back in time."

They looked up at the tree, starting well above Sam's head and ending at our feet. I pointed out Noah ("Remember the big boat?") and then followed the colored lines that ran down the tree, pointing out the lineage of the three religions.

"See? Here's Moses. And then you follow this, and there's Jesus—the baby from wintertime? And here, here's Mohammed. See how they're connected? They just have different books. Even those are interconnected. That's what this says—despite all the conflict, they are all worshipping the same god. They just differ on the details. They all came from the same place. They are part of the same family."

I had tears in my eyes. My voice was cracking. I wished more people could experience what we had those past few days. I wished they could stand there before that giant family diagram through time and remember they were all related—connected. We all are.

Samaire grabbed my hand, watching my tears fall.

"So these are just more stories to help people live their lives the best they can? Like the Greek gods?"

I stopped and stared at her and then grabbed her fiercely and hugged her to me.

"Yes, my love," I whispered in her ear. "They all believe their stories are as real as the Greeks did. It helps remind them what's important."

I might be stumbling through this parenting fiasco, but every once in a while, Sam and I get something right. If Samaire can understand somehow that religions and their related stories are really all about helping different people find a way to live their best lives, she's going to be okay. It's not about answers, just guideposts.

We left Turkey and headed to Greece, where we wandered the maze of the Minotaur and danced in Zeus's temple beneath never-ending stars to a live swing band. We told stories. We shared myths. We touched the places where the myths began.

I can't give them all the answers. I don't believe "all the answers" even exists. What I can do is show them how I live my life, what I believe, and give them the context as much as possible of everything else. They will write their own stories someday, find their own path. I can't give them a bracelet of commandments or a community with answers at the ready, but I can give them guidance. I can point them in a good direction. I can give them people who love them and who appreciate the mystery, too.

I will give them their own stories. I will empower them in their ongoing legends as they build them.

The myths and fables I give my children are never just about teaching right versus wrong or even how I believe the world works. Above all, these narratives are ways I can help them learn to discover their own unique tales, ways to put words and meaning to the voice that speaks to them from within their heart. I want them to know that the most powerful, the most meaningful stories originate within themselves: in their brave souls, their curious minds, their hopeful hearts. The world creates stories of its own, but the ones that matter are the ones they create.

These personal mythologies I create for them now are often a way of trying to protect them, as well, from the narratives that may damage their precious psyches and spirits. If they can feel the genuine power of their own truths, if they can see that no one outside themselves has the one undeniable answer, perhaps they'll be less susceptible to other people's judgment, to the narratives others will try to write them into. Perhaps in some small way, the stories we weave together now will lend them strength and courage down the road, will somehow amplify the wondrous tales already growing inside them. I can only hope. Some of those outside stories are powerfully dogged at times.

The world will teach Samaire soon enough about languishing princesses and their saving prince, about tulle and crowns, about pink and polka dots. It will show her shoes with impossibly high heels to wear, dresses with useless endless trains—it will drown her in fairy tales. It will burden Wylie with dragons and castles and swords. It will give him no room to cry or show weakness; it will make demands on his heart no one should have to endure. It will smother him in steel.

I will give my daughter this: I will give her the blue of the sky, the gold of the sun, even the brown of the earth. I will dirty her toes and smudge her cheeks; I will tangle her hair in the wind and roughen her hands in dirt. I will show her she is no princess, but a child of the universe. A creation. A creator.

I will teach my son the names of every flower, and we will drown in the beauty of the stars. I will give him the softness of snow and the wild of winter. I will cover him in clover, and we will count the breaths it takes for the sun to disappear behind the horizon. We will cry together over the beauty and wonder of the world, and I will show him he is not all sharp corners and harsh edges. He is made not of metal and weapons and brashness but the wind and the tides and the stars.

It is all I have for them, all I can give. It might not be enough.

But there it is, somehow. We stumble through. I give them stories of their own, stories of traditions and gods and goddesses the eras have passed down to us, tied to each sacred day we celebrate. I give them stories of where we came from and who the people were who came before us. And I give them stories I make up, to teach them to value their own ways of figuring out how to live their best life, stories to let them know they are always loved, that they should always love. Stories to remind them of their own power, their own greatness, and their own importance.

One of Wylie's favorite stories is one he now retells on a regular basis, regarding the moon. When he was small, Wylie had a fascination with the moon, or "Moona," as he called her. We would look out our window every night as we rocked to sleep to find her. When we walked outside as the sun set and the handful of stars we could see began to peek out, I would call attention to how she followed always above us, always behind. He reveled in it. Finding Moona in the sky became a game we played whenever possible, and soon he was asking why she would follow us. *Why is Moona always over me when the sun sets?*

Ah, the moon. I have a special affinity for the moon, as I've explained, and I adored that Wylie was fascinated with her. And so he got a story of his own.

My darling boy, when you were born, it took us all night and into the early morning to get to hold you. We were worried for you, and when you were finally in my arms, I thought I would cry with joy. To finally have you safe with me, to hold you and know you were real and alive and healthy . . . it meant the whole world to me. I leaned back and held your small head to my chest so you could hear my heart, in hopes you would somehow know how happy I was in that moment. As I held you there, one of the nurses pulled open the curtain over the window across from us, and there I saw the faintest shadow of what was left of the moon in the sky.

Part of me felt like the moon had been waiting eagerly for you, too.

So I looked out that window and asked her to please always watch over you: to greet you every night when you needed to be reminded how much you are loved, to shine bright on you when I wasn't close by to hold you myself. I asked the moon to look after you always, just as she looked over you that morning.

Now, as you search for her in the night sky, you can know she is always there to remind you that you are not alone. Just as I will always love you, she will always look over you. Even when you can't see her, when the shadow of the earth hides her, she is still there among the stars—just like even when I can't be with you, my love is still yours.

It's just a small silly story, but it's one he and I share. We sing songs about the moon together, we search for her still on our walks. It's not much, but it's something I hope he can always carry with him, like the hearts I used to draw on his hand when he was scared to go to school.

We all have our stories. What I've found I truly love is that so many of them overlap. We're all just trying to live and love our best.

Sam and I are constantly having conversations about how we can be better parents. I had never quite understood, until it happened, what a tremendously frightening thing being a parent would be. For the first month, I was just desperate to somehow keep this tiny creature alive. We monitored all the signs of health. We kept track of hours slept, diapers changed. Then we moved into trying to keep them from hurting themselves, covering sharp corners, following along behind toddling, drunken-stepping little people, ready to catch them or quickly move something out of the way as they explored their new world.

And now, just when it feels like we have that part down—at least for Samaire; I feel I shall forever be worried about whatever Wylie might attempt physically that will put him in inevitable terminal danger—we face a whole new, seemingly insurmountable challenge: How do I teach my kids bravery? Not the kind required to swing higher or run a bit farther, not the kind that has them jumping into the pool with smiles on their faces or standing on the stage singing a song they've practiced all week for a part in the school play. I'm worried about the kind of bravery that runs steadily beneath all of that, the kind they will need as they navigate this world—partly, and simply, because their mom is a witch.

As most of us are well aware, being different often invites derision. Our world, as much as I want to see it as an open and loving and welcoming place, often falls short. People need very little impetus to be cruel, and religion is sadly (and ironically) often the arena in which some feel authorized to be the cruelest. Hell is not a small or idle threat. Stereotypes, as much as I make light of them, can be an all too welcoming platform on which to raise unkindness.

Until I had them, I never truly considered how my choice of beliefs could haunt my children. It had caught up to me a time or two; I had already been unfriended on Facebook by my uncle's wife because I openly stated I was pagan. It wasn't the first time people had faded from my life because of that fact, nor would it be the last. However, that was just me. I have peace in my heart over the choices I have made. I made them knowing there might be consequences, and I accept them. I have no interest in changing who I am, what I believe, for someone else's comfort or righteousness.

However, the first time it occurred to me that my children would pay a price for this decision I had made, the peace I had in my heart was undeniably shaken. My friend Sarah had a baby not long after I had Samaire, and she and I were talking about how sometimes being a parent alters your immediate circle of friendship, through no other cause than a lack of time or energy or conflicting schedules. Then she mentioned she had recently put distance between herself and a mutual friend of a friend for another child-induced reason: "He believes my children are going to hell because I didn't have them baptized."

It felt like someone had punched me in the gut. I looked down at the precious, perfect being in my arms and realized that someday I would have to explain to her that there were people in this world—people we knew (people we were *related* to, even)—who believed that her mama would go to hell when she died. Who believed *she* would spend eternity in damnation if she did not leave behind everything I had taught her was true as a child. I could hear suddenly in my head all the corner preachers, see all the signs held up in public parks, the pamphlets handed out on subway platforms, even the ridiculous memes online—all the things, large and small, I had learned to let go of, to ignore. They all felt dangerous now to this new soul in my care.

In the grand scheme of things, I know I don't have so much to fear. My children will not be persecuted; they won't be hunted. They live in a place where they have the freedom to worship as they wish. They may hear the occasional unkind word, encounter the sporadic fervent recruiter. If I raise them right, they will learn to turn their backs to those who cannot accept them for who they are—*all* of who they are. But even the slightest sting that might cause them breaks my heart nonetheless.

I've made a multitude of decisions regarding my kids and on behalf of my kids that turned out to be less than optimal. There have been days we've pushed them a little bit farther than we should have, dragging them from one place to another until they were so exhausted that we all paid with a brilliant and fantastic meltdown (mine *and* theirs, mine *or* theirs; it's all happened, to be fair). And there was the time Samaire and Wylie both bring up with some regularity when Sam and I chose *Batman vs. Dracula* for our screening on family movie night. We had watched all the other Batman cartoons available, and this one seemed as innocuous as the rest—but instead, it was absolutely terrifying. Both children begged us to turn it off, only it was so absolutely frightening we made them finish it for fear that if they didn't know how it all ended the consequences would be even worse. So we sat, Sam and I each holding a quivering child in our lap as we watched the epic battle unfold. I'm positive Sam was the only one who slept well that night. (Though, if I remember correctly, even he paid the price, as both kids eventually landed in bed with me and Sam ended up folded up on the couch for lack of room in our pile of sleepy fear.)

So I have plenty of experience making questionable parenting choices. I'd like to say my Wiccan beliefs unfailingly guide me as a centered and self-aware woman through the pitfalls of motherhood, but that would be an all-out lie. I fall prey to the trappings of exhaustion and impatience and simple distraction as often as the next person. I forget to pack lunches or make sure the lunch containers seal properly. I forget the birthday parties. I forget to check the rating on a Batman cartoon. I forget almost as often as I remember.

But on the whole, I do feel like I might be getting it right slightly more often than I get it wrong. (Look, I'm not swinging for the majors here. A girl's gotta know her league.) I know the world is full of cruelty and apathy. I know that different isn't always seen as better, and one decision I have made for my children that I really worry about is making them different. Oh, I know there are worse things—worse than having a witch as your mom, worse than being a practicing pagan, at least until or if they decide to be otherwise. I get it, but it doesn't stop the worry from burrowing into my heart.

This past year, for Valentine's Day, we did our nails. Samaire picked pinks and reds for her nails, I painted mine maroon, and Wylie asked to paint his Superman blue. We sat on the couch while I gave them manicures and we watched *How to Train Your Dragon* and had a wonderful night. The next morning, we surprised them with new books and sent them off to school, excited for all the fun yet to be had.

When I got home and asked how their days were, Wylie answered, "Horrible. The boys joked on me for my fingers."

I felt as if I had been punched in the gut. I immediately scooped him up and listened to the details as I crafted a scathing letter to the teacher at his after-school program in my head. Sam could see the steam pouring out of my ears and went on to have Wylie tell me how Daddy had already talked to him and how when they went to get Samaire at her school, so many teachers and students complimented him that he didn't feel so bad anymore.

But, was all I could think. *But*. But he had to feel what he felt as those boys teased him still. It might not have been long, and Sam was able to fix it . . . *but*. I felt so guilty for not anticipating that he would be teased, and then I felt torn because he *liked* his nails painted Superman blue. He always has. Shouldn't I teach him that he should be himself no matter what? To be proud?

I worry, as my kids get older, that my decisions about how we talk about our beliefs and what we actually teach them will affect them in the same way as me painting Wylie's nails blue. Despite the fact that it was a good lesson for him to learn—"Mama, Daddy said those other boys were just mean because they are jealous, or sad. I can't let them stop me from being happy and doing things I like. People who are mean like that aren't my friends"—it killed me that he had to hurt, even for a second, over something I had encouraged him to do. Yet, there I was. Here I am.

We have also had minor incidents at school from time to time. Once, Samaire cried in her preschool class because when they studied how stories were put together, everyone listed witches as the bad guys, itemized under the "antagonist" column. She wanted them on the hero side of the list, too, but no one would agree to that. Her tears flowed as she sat on her little rug, uncharacteristically silent, through the rest of the lesson. Her teacher asked me about it when I picked her up, confused as to why it had been so important and wondering if perhaps she didn't quite understand what they had been talking about. It seemed out of the norm to her; Samaire was usually a quick study, and this story unit had seemed to be one of her favorites. I told her that of course Samaire understood, but her mom was a witch. She wanted me to be a hero . . . or at least not just a villain. When I talked to Samaire, she understood—*People don't usually know the kind of witch Mama is; they only know the wicked ones from stories. Just remind them of the good ones, too*—And we got through it fairly unscathed.

During a spat of some kind, another boy called Wylie a witch (ignorant of how it might actually apply) in that same teacher's class, years later. This was much less of an issue, as Wylie just became confused as to why the boy got in trouble. He couldn't understand why calling him a witch was bad, and the teacher couldn't quite understand why Wylie was so unfazed and unmoved by her explanation. When I walked up to the door to pick him up that day, she smiled at me and said, "Ah, now I remember," and told me what had happened. We laughed about it, and I walked Wylie home. I spoke to Wylie about how the intention of words is often more important than the actual words themselves, and how we always must speak with kindness and respect. That lack of kindness was why his classmate had been in trouble. We moved on.

Both times the incidents were not a big deal. Both times they weren't hurtful as much as they were confusing. They were easily resolved. But

I fear the day when that may not be the case; I ache over it already. I know logically that there will always be a reason for someone to tease my children, that if someone chooses to be mean or dislike them, they will find a reason to suit their purpose. I just hate the idea that it could be a reason I provided.

We do our best to steel our children for a world that often doesn't value what's different as good or beautiful or unique but rather as frightening. We explain how a person's belief system can be very dear to them and that we must always, always respect it. I talk to them about how we can never know what's in someone's heart, and more often than not, people won't understand what's in ours. The world makes a lot of assumptions. I don't know how to protect them from that, so I try to break the assumptions. I try to speak up and speak out. I try to teach Wylie and Samaire to do the same on behalf of things that are important to them. We tell them the best thing we can do as people is learn about one another with open hearts.

We read them books, we take them on trips, we show them that the beauty of the world is its diversity. We tell them they are loved. We try to teach them about what's important through our actions. We support them; we let them know they always have a safe place. As a parent, I might never get it absolutely right, but who does? We are all stumbling through this world blindly, hoping our best will be good enough. It may not be, but at the very least I hope my children will look back and know I tried. I keep painting Wylie's nails blue and telling Samaire stories that have good witches.

AND WE'LL DANCE BY THE LIGHT OF THE MOON

LIKE ANY OTHER RELIGION, WICCA HAS "HOLY" DAYS: DAYS WHEN Wiccans pause and recognize and remember, days when it is imperative to take a moment to honor our place on the wheel of life as it turns, to hold ourselves accountable for our place within that greater mechanism and remember that we are just one small part of it, connected to all that surrounds us. These days remind us we are part of a great web of life, an intricate pattern, and we belong to a larger story. They offer a chance for us to honor the passing of time and the natural rhythms by which we live.

Unsurprisingly, then, those days fall around natural occurrences: solstices, equinoxes, and phases of the moon. They mark the passage of time and act as indicators of ceremony, both large and small. Beginning a new job or project, or building a new habit, as the moon builds in the sky reminds me the world is growing with me. The universe, in all its power, accompanies me. I want to feel in tune with the world around me; I revel in the idea of being a part of something so wonderful and grand as I learn and evolve.

You will often hear Wiccans refer to the "Wheel"; I have referenced it a couple times already. This is a reference to the Wheel of Life, the ongoing progression we are all lucky enough to be part of and connected to. Often the term is also used in reference to the Wheel of the Year, the cycle of seasons. Wiccans recognize each "turn of the wheel" as a milestone in the earth's journey around the sun. There are eight of these, called Sabbats. They recognize each equinox, each solstice, and the points midway between, known as cross-quarter days. These are our most sacred days. Each holds special meaning, tied to the relative dominance of light and dark throughout the year. Sabbats are a chance to recognize our place amid the grandeur of the universe we live in and to consciously reconnect with the natural cycles of the world around us.

The Sabbats begin the night before at sunset and carry forward through sunset the next day. One fun fact: because the holidays are based on seasonal cycles, pagans in the Northern and Southern Hemispheres celebrate the holidays opposite each other. When one half of the world is observing Samhain, for example, the other half is rejoicing in Beltane.

When I first started practicing, I was afraid I would miss the holidays that defined my year in my previous life. I was afraid the absence of those touchstones would leave me drifting. What I soon discovered was that I had been celebrating many of the Wiccan Sabbats already by relishing the onset of each new season, and a good deal of my "new" holiday traditions coincided nicely with my previous celebrations. I missed nothing. I was able to keep a lot of the traditions that meant the most to me while finally finding a rhythm to the year that felt right.

These holidays help me to recognize what is important. Like any other person, I have my years when certain holidays sneak up on me and our house is turned upside down by last-minute grocery runs and meals out of boxes, when I grab candles and try to impart the most meaning I can with what time we have between homework packets and late-night work calls. That said, I do revel in each one. I have found these turns of the wheel speak to me, to how I inevitably feel at each gateway to the next revolution. I find peace and joy in each day and ritual, and as our family grows together, the days become more precious each year.

In the following pages, I describe the way my family and I celebrate and attach meaning to each of the Sabbats. Not every witch will view them the same way or have similar traditions. However, the overall themes should be similar enough that you get a feel for what is being honored and revered as the wheel turns and we recognize the days that ask us to stop and take notice.

I am going to go through the holidays as we would through the year, starting with our "new year," Samhain. You might be more familiar with the holiday most celebrated at that time of year: Halloween. We might as well start off as witchily as possible, right?

SAMHAIN

I want to tell you that Samhain is this lovely, honored holiday in our calendar—that my children garner meaning from it that surpasses the uncomplicated joy of candy and costumes and general calamity.

But I can't, simply because it's not true.

Halloween is *huge* for our family. We all dress up, and we do so multiple times. We celebrate with my parents and close friends at Disney World's Not-So-Scary Halloween Party every Columbus Day weekend. At home, we also have the various after-school-program parties and actual-school dress-up days, plus the evening of Halloween itself, when we wander the avenues, the kids with their bags outstretched, yelling, "Trick or Treat!" as they run wildly and purposefully through the doors of the restaurants, bodegas, and smoke shops of our neighborhood.

Like all parents, Sam and I try to balance the safety rule of "Don't talk to strangers" with encouraging flat-out panhandling for a night. "Say thank you, even if there's no candy!" "Don't forget to hold the door for the kids behind you!" "Don't complain about what you get! Be grateful!!" I spend all night cajoling and yelling as I chase my children from doorway to doorway, stoop to stoop. In all the madness, not once will you hear me yell, "Merry Samhain! Brightest blessings!!" The closest I may get to a blessing is when we're halfway through the night and the guy behind the counter at Schmackary's offers me a free cookie once the kids have picked out theirs. *That* guy will get blessings for sure—and maybe a kiss straight on the mouth.

So yes, despite the hullabaloo over all the supposed demon worshipping happening that night, I am setting the bar low for witchcraft. No Ouija board for me, no tarot layout. I, much like all of you, am carrying the masks that everyone had to have but no one wants to wear and trailing along behind my brood, stealing miniature Kit Kats along the way. I do always manage to take a moment at the end of the night to thank the gods that we all got through—and cheerfully so—as I watch my children separate and count their sugarific haul.

So, do we celebrate Samhain at all? Has it anything to do with Halloween or the traditions around it? Yes and no. Our family's celebration of Samhain comes the night before Halloween, when things are a bit more quiet and the night still (though generally Samhain will more likely officially fall on October 31 or November 1-ish). It begins that morning, as I gather the right foods from the fridge and my daughter and I search through old cookbooks and loose notes in looped, cramped handwriting.

Our Samhain is about stories and traditions, and all who have come before. It honors all those we have loved who are no longer with us. For that day, we choose to begin to embrace the darkness of the coming winter and the sadness that comes with remembering those we have lost. We tell their stories, we laugh at their jokes. We eat their food and listen to their music. We relish in what they gave us, what they left behind—and for just a few moments, they are there with us. The veil between this world and the next, the thin line between today and yesterday, dissipates, and we share their love, their presence, if only for a little while.

Of course, our Samhain is just that—ours. As you well know by now, Wiccans all do this differently. However, there are definite running themes and traditions (not the least of which is that request for treats or tricks).

Samhain (pronounced "*Sah*-wen" or "*Sow*-in") lands almost exactly between the autumn equinox and the winter solstice. It marks the beginning of fall and the coming of the darkest part of the year. It is often celebrated on or near Halloween. Some witches will celebrate it on the nearest full moon, or in the beginning of November, closer to the actual astronomical midpoint between the equinox and solstice.

Regardless of when the actual celebration takes place, Samhain is rich in legend and lore, mysticism and magic. Samhain marks the beginning of a new year—a moment when we are suspended in time between what is behind us and what lies ahead. It belongs neither to the coming nor the passing year. The ancient Celts believed that the night preceded the day, and so the dark of the year preceded the light; a new year begins as the darkness creeps in. It is a time of reflection and hope, of reminiscence and anticipation. It is a night to breathe, to be released of expectation and to simply be grateful in the moment for all that has passed and all that is yet to come.

Samhain is the last harvest festival, on the cusp of winter. Summer has ended, winter not quite yet begun. Because of this, it holds a special sort of magic. It lies between years—between worlds.

Samhain is when the normal laws that bind us loosen, when the veil between the reality we live in and all that we don't know dissipates. For one night, we stand in the gray between life and death; we pause in a timeless place and are able to live a waking dream. We consider the dark nights to come and let go of the hot days that brought us here. We recognize that what is ahead awaits our work and strength, waits for us to define it—while everything and everyone that came before laid the path that led us here.

And so, Samhain is about darkness and about ghosts and saints and demons, in a way. But there is nothing in the darkness to fear—isn't the dark of the soil where the seed sprouts roots? Is it not in the darkness beneath his mother's heart that a child grows? The dark part of the year is a time for reflection and plan making. It's when we take the time to care for ourselves and nurture our hopes and dreams so we can be ready to take action when the light comes again.

That being the case, the ghosts we see on Samhain aren't about hauntings or a fearsome summoning. In the same way that we shouldn't fear the darkness, we also accept and reflect on those who came before us: the ones who lent us their genes for our eyes and short temper, our athletic prowess or love of poetry, the traits both good and bad. We all have relatives we'd like to ignore, but they have contributed to who we are, too. Every experience, every anecdote that precedes us strengthens and defines us.

And as for those we wish we *could* bring back? Those who came before us and left too soon, those whom we never got to meet but whose stories live on brilliantly and vibrantly—what about them? Who doesn't know the pull on your heart when you suddenly reach for someone who is no longer there, the emptiness felt in the very center of your chest that you carry with you like an echo of their presence? Yet there's the moment your son smiles at you and you see his grandfather, there is your daughter's laughter that echoes the mirth of her great aunt. There are those fleeting, almost imperceptible instants when for a split second those loved ones are there with you, when what you've lost comes crashing back.

Samhain is a chance to intentionally create those moments: to welcome the memories back in, to push through the sadness of the loss and celebrate what was given. It's a holiday to honor those we have lost, those we miss, those we ache for. It's a chance to consciously call up the memories we so often pack away and share them, to bring back those we love, if only for the length of a dinner, a movie, a song.

More often than not, at Samhain you will find us crowded around one of the many family cookbooks we have collected over the years. The kids and I will pore over our options, and Sam and I will more than likely spend as much time telling stories of the people who first made those meals as actually cooking them. We will tell stories of what we ate as kids, the meals we shared with our families. We will sing the praises of Uncle Phil's beignets (they may have been from a box, but waking up to the smell of them first thing in the morning made them five star) and mourn the loss of Grandma Alice's pumpkin pie. Some recipes just will never be the same.

We will tell stories that go far beyond the ingredients and directions scribbled and typed on page after page of greased paper, so thin with the handling of generations it is almost see-through. I will get lost down the rabbit hole of memory, telling stories the kids have heard a thousand times and will hear a thousand more, stories they can now tell forward and backward about people they never met, yet now somehow remember. Those people are real to Samaire and Wylie because we tell their stories, we make their bread, and we sing their songs. The people we love, the ones who have touched us, haven't gone so far away—not when we take the time to hold their memory close and share their amazing stories.

So, yes, I suppose Samhain has its share of ghosts and spirits. They just aren't conjured by a game board's alphabet or a magic spell. But they are welcomed in and celebrated; we open our home to their tales and relive what we can of their memories. We toast with their favorite drinks and pass around their favorite dishes. We pause—every time—when we skip the empty place we have set, the single chair that reminds us not only of all who have gone before but that our time, too, is fleeting.

We light candles to remember how fragile the light can be and to prepare for the dark of the year. At our house, more often than not, those candles are ensconced in pumpkins, a tradition more Halloween than Samhain. The two holidays are absolutely intrinsically tied and yet still worlds apart. That's what happens with a lot of my holidays: they echo of the familiar, but they run their own course.

Our meal for Samhain is always the same: beef stew. The recipe is a combination of bits and pieces of other recipes handed down through our families and the first solid-food meal Wylie ever ate. It reminds me of home—what it should be, warm and welcoming and rich in all the ways that matter. It also reminds me that time passes so very fast. It feels like just yesterday Wylie was in his high chair, with all of us crowded around oohing and ahhing over this milestone. Time plays tricks, speeding up only to come to an abrupt stop. Making this stew lets me slow down a bit, reminds me it's okay to take all day to just revel in what we have.

Alongside the stew, I like to serve rosemary bread. Rosemary has been used for magic, healing, and seasoning since the beginnings of recorded history. Ancient Greeks and Romans revered it as a symbol of love and death and remembrance; they used rosemary in wedding ceremonies to help the bride and groom remember their vows. Ancient Egyptians used rosemary as part of their embalming ceremonies, and it has long been placed at tombs as a promise to remember loved ones who have passed. As we make our bread we tell the stories of our favorite relatives who are no longer with us. We try to imbue the dough with the love, laughter, and gifts they gave us that we carry to this day.

Roasted Garlic Rosemary Bread

2   heads roasted garlic
1   cup warm water (not boiling)
1   packet active dry yeast (¼ ounce)
2   teaspoons white sugar
2   teaspoons fine salt
3   tablespoons extra-virgin olive oil
2 ½ cups bread flour
1   tablespoon dried, chopped rosemary leaves
¼   teaspoon freshly ground black pepper
    Fresh rosemary leaves torn from the stem
    Additional herbs

The first order of business is to roast the garlic. This is my favorite part; I adore roasted garlic. I also freely admit that the amount I'm recommending in this recipe might be a bit overboard for some people. Maybe. Perhaps it's my grandfather Carlotta's Sicilian roots. Either way, knock off some of the extra papery skin from the heads and cut off the tips of the bulbs while the oven preheats to 400–450 degrees Fahrenheit. Then put each of those delicious bulbs on a flat of aluminum foil, drizzle them with olive oil, and sprinkle with sea salt and pepper. Pinch and twist the corners of the foil around the bulb, making little packets, and throw them right into the oven. Keep them in there about 30–35 minutes or until they feel soft.

When you take them out, let them cool enough to touch and then squeeze the garlic out of the cloves into a small bowl. I find it easier to pinch them out of the bulb while it's still pretty warm, but, you know, use common sense. The last thing you want is to create a not-so-great memory of burned fingers to relive every year.

Then I take our large avocado-green Pyrex bowl that was once Sam's mother's and pour in one cup of warm water. (Take the time to revel a bit in your hand-me-downs. Recognize them for the love they contained when given and the love they held long before you held them. We always take a moment to appreciate the endless bowls of his favorite Chex mix that Grammy made just for Daddy in this very bowl. We tell the kids how she gave him the bowl when he got his own home, so he could still have homemade Chex mix, even if she couldn't always make it for him.) Be sure the water is just warm, not hot. Carefully combine the yeast, sugar, and salt into a small container, then sprinkle into the water. (This is fun for the kids to do, as it should bubble when the mixture hits the water.) Leave it be for approximately 10 minutes or until it gets nice and foamy.

Pour the olive oil into the water mixture and then add the flour. I always feel I have to fold in the flour in batches, but this probably makes no difference whatsoever. Then mix it all together with your hands for about 10 minutes. It should get to the point, fairly quickly, where you'll end up being able to knead it. If it gets too sticky on the bowl, go ahead and add a little olive oil or flour to your counter and work there. I find it also works nicely to add a bit to your hands.

Add in dried rosemary and black pepper as you work the dough. This is where you can add additional herbs if you'd like; I often throw in a few pinches of oregano. Oregano is used for happiness, tranquility, luck, health, and protection, but is especially relevant to this bread as it is also supposed to help you let go of a loved one and banish sadness. I like to think it helps us let go of the sadness of remembering and relive the joy of what was. You could also add basil for sympathy, or thyme for healing—whatever sounds good. Go crazy and add a pinch of an Italian spice mix to cover all your bases. I won't tell.

After another 5 minutes of kneading, gently add in half the roasted garlic. Mix in for another minute. The dough should be a pretty solid structure at this point and might be a bit sticky. Bring it into a ball shape and place it in a well-oiled bowl, turning it a few times so that it has a nice thin layer of oil all around it. Cover the bowl tightly and place in a warm, draft-free area to rise. The dough should double in about an hour. Don't freak out too much if that doesn't happen, just give it another hour—or lose track of time like I do and let two hours go by. Either way, it will be fine.

This next part is the kids' favorite: Now that the dough has doubled, punch it down, then take it out of the bowl and place it on a greased baking sheet. Round it into a somewhat loaf-looking shape, or whatever shape seems best. Just make sure it's more roundish than square-ish. Little hands will require oil on them so they don't stick too much.

Using a sharp knife, carve a design into the top of the loaf. You can do a normal cross-cross design, or get fancy with a pentacle or heart or even your family's initial. Then you need to cover the dough one more time. I find a large mixing bowl turned upside down works nicely, but use whatever works and is handy. Our Pyrex bowl seems to fit perfectly. If there's too much dough for just one of your bowls, you can always make two smaller loaves. Just make sure the dough has room to rise.

It will double once more in about an hour.

Once it's doubled again, you can brush it with olive oil or mix some of your leftover roasted garlic with butter. After you're done adding some moisture to the top of the dough, it's the perfect time to sprinkle with sea salt, some fresh rosemary leaves, and whatever other herbs might tickle your fancy. Throw the loaf in the oven at 375 degrees for about half an hour. Then, if you want a nice crusty top, spray it with water and bump up the temperature to 425. Bake it until the top turns a nice golden brown, usually just another 5 minutes or so. I fully admit to lightly hitting the loaf with more oil or butter on that last round instead of water, but do what feels right. For an extra bump, brush some melted butter and sprinkle just a bit of salt or even parmesan cheese for a bit of yummy added taste and texture.

Once done, you should have delicious bread to dip into your stew.

Every family has some sort of stew recipe, I imagine, the kind that uses up whatever is in the cupboards and provides some warmth when the weather starts to cool. It's the kind of recipe with a lot of clauses: *If you don't have this, use that.* The making itself becomes the recipe after a while, cards and papers long left behind as each family cook adds their own spin to its creation. This is ours.

BELL-STIERS BEEF STEW

2	tablespoons butter
2	pounds cubed beef
	Salt and pepper
1 ½	cups flour
2	small red onions, sliced
2	tablespoons tomato paste
1	small squeeze anchovy paste
8	cloves of garlic, minced
¾	bottle beer (any ale, stout, or dark beer will work)
7–10	ounces beef broth
	Cumin
1	bay leaf
8	red potatoes, quartered
1	package green peas
	Avocado

Preheat your oven to 350 degrees Fahrenheit. Put two tablespoons of butter in the bottom of a Dutch oven or any somewhat large, deep, heavy pot. As it heats over a medium-high flame, season the beef with salt and pepper, then toss in flour. (You can roll it in flour on a plate or throw the flour in a Ziploc bag and then toss the beef cubes inside.) Drop the beef in batches into the pot and brown it on all sides. Be careful not to overfill the pot when you do each batch, as it makes it difficult to turn the cubes.

Once they're all nice and browned on the outside, return all the beef to the pot and add in the sliced onions. Turn the heat down to medium and let the onions soften.

While the delicious aroma of beef and onions fills your kitchen, find a small bowl. Mix together the tomato paste, the anchovy paste, and the minced garlic. Once it's nice and mixed up, throw it all into the pot.

The stew should start to smell super good. When it's deliciously smell-y, after about 3 minutes, slowly pour in the beer. (Don't quite use the whole bottle; instead, toast those you're remembering and drink the last few swallows. No Samhain meal, or any meal really, is complete without at least a couple of toasts.) Stir a bit, scraping the bottom of the pan to lift up the yummy bits stuck there. Then add the beef broth. Depending on how soupy you like your stew, you can add more or less broth. I like to reserve a few ounces and make that call after it's all cooked.

Speaking of, to keep it nice and thick and more "stew" than "soup," add in the extra half cup of flour. Stir it in well, until none of the white of the flour is visible. Once it's well combined, add in the cumin to taste. We love it, so I always add a solid tablespoon (or, more honestly, a bunch of shakes. So many shakes), and I'd suggest at least two teaspoons. Add some more salt and pepper, drop in the bay leaf, and let the whole pot simmer for 15–20 minutes until it all starts to thicken.

Once it's thickening, top the stew with a lid and put it in the oven for an hour and a half. Conveniently, this is about the same length of time as a movie, so you can always grab Poppy's favorite musical and have a family sing-along while you wait. The options are endless. And fun.

After you've enjoyed some quality family time, add in the quartered potatoes. Stir well, then put back in the oven. This is an excellent time to break out some scrapbooks and home videos.

After 45 minutes, take the pot out of the oven and add in the peas. Simmer for just 10 more minutes. At this point, your house should smell amazing. Go ahead and grab some big spoons and some hunks of rosemary bread and sit down over a nice bowl of comfort food. We always like to top the stew with hunks of avocado, but you do you.

Yule (Winter Solstice)

Yule, or the winter solstice, falls at the beginning of our spiritual year and the end of our calendar one. It always seems to hit me right as the dark mornings, gray evenings, and hectic pace of the larger holidays surrounding it feel as if they are about to drag me under.

Longest night of the year, indeed.

Every year I feel as if I collapse at the feet of Yule. The darkness of the days pulls at something deep in my chest, and I find even normal activities can be challenging. Yet rarely are there only normal activities happening. Inevitably, the run from Samhain to Yule is filled with the typical end-of-year marathon of work deadlines, school projects and special activities, family plans, and get-togethers—all wonderful, and all wonderfully exhausting.

Yet it is absolutely fitting that Yule should come right when I feel I might fall apart. Yule is a holiday filled with hope and light. Its entire purpose is to have us stop and bask in the coming of illumination to our world, a chance to crawl out of the darkness and stand in the coming sun. Truth be told, Yule is not so different from many of the other religious holidays being celebrated at the end of our calendar year. Yule is a celebration of the renewed birth of the sun, the idea that in the dark of our souls there sparks a new hope—a sacred fire, the light of the world—if only we take the time to nurture it.

While Christians ready themselves for the birth of their light of the world and Jews honor the miraculous light of Maccabee, we witches say good-bye to the darkness and light fires of our own. We stop and take a breath. We recognize that we have survived the darkness and hopefully look back to see we flourished in it. We welcome in the light and begin to make plans of action. While the darkness is perfect to set plans to seed, the coming light spurs action. It is time to wake from the dream and begin living it.

We take stock and set aside the things we want to leave behind: the actions and words, plans and programs best left in the darkness. We face the sun and the hope in front of us and decide how best we can contribute to the growing light around us.

As a family, a lot of our customs around Yule go hand in hand with many mainstream customs associated with Christmas. We exchange gifts on Yule, but we make a point to be sure they are handmade or are experiences we can share together as a family. We light candles, and I decorate our home with as many lights as Sam will agree to hang. We bring in evergreen boughs, even a tree, to remind us of the constancy of the goddess and the promise of new growth in the coming months.

We turn on the Yule log on the television and write out our hopes for the year on small pieces of paper. We write how we will bring those hopes to fruition. Then we take those small slips of paper, those beginnings, and give them up to the fire and light. We set them in a cauldron, where we watch them burn and be the light we aspire to become in the coming months. It's a time of hope. There is the possibility of great growth and change in all of us, and on this night, we celebrate its emergence.

There's no missing, however, the season in which Yule falls. It is impossible to celebrate the winter solstice without acknowledging that it happens in the midst of the Christmas season. There's no escaping it. It's in the specials on the television, the soundtrack in the stores, the lights up in the neighborhood, the greetings of everyone from friends to neighbors to strangers on the street. Yule falls a scant few days ahead of the Big One—you know, that holiday I spent every year of my childhood counting down the days to. And for all the traditions and ceremonies and rituals and answers I may have given up for my new faith, I have a confession to make:

I did not give up Christmas.

Oh no, I did not. My completely pagan heart falls in love every time with the hope the end of the calendar year brings, and winter holidays for me last from the solstice straight through Christmas Day. Then there it is: not just the idea of a holiday, but Christmas itself in full regalia filling our home. I freely admit this might be a bit confusing—I mean, Sam and I are pagans. There is no denying it, no shying away from it, and it is how we are raising our children. There is no Easter for them, no All Saints' Day. How do we explain the sudden onslaught of Christian wintertime tradition in our home?

Sure, instead of a crèche we have a Rudolph scene complete with not one but *four* Bumbles and three Jedi. But the music I begin playing on Thanksgiving afternoon is almost impossible to explain away. I mean, I love me some holidays, and while our "true" holiday is the solstice, one our family celebrates with full rigmarole and a joyous sense of occasion, I simply cannot give up Christmas morning. Or carols. (All the other stuff I could keep, as it was all evolved from pagan traditions to begin with. But the "Silent Nights" and "God Rest Ye's"—there's really no getting around that.)

To me, it's quite simple. I'm not celebrating the birth of a savior, a god's only son. I'm not celebrating all that entails, and by the look of the general marketplace, neither are a lot of other people. I am, however, celebrating the birth of a child, and the hope that surrounded that child. Christmas, to me, is not so different from Yule: it is about the sheer wonder a great part of the world showed (shows) in celebrating the birth of one small, helpless child. Just as Yule celebrates the tenacity of a world that will not give up in the midst of darkness, a world prepared to welcome in the light, Christmas reminds my family of the idea that each of us holds the power to be that light.

I love the story. It's one I gladly share with our children every year, one I feel is vital they hear as we look toward months of becoming a light in the darkness ourselves.

A small family—not royal, not famous, not rich—expects a child, under circumstances that aren't ideal. They do their best to prepare; they do their best to be safe. And while they are trying desperately to keep it together—to make a home, a safe respite, for their tiny blessing—something else happens. The news spreads. Kings lift up their scabbards, robes, and scepters and begin traveling to where they believe the baby will be found. Small groups of shepherds herd their flocks to be near; people gather—all kinds of people from all kinds of places. They gather with hope in their hearts, anticipation in their souls.

They believe that this baby will change the world. Make it better. Make it brighter. Bring them light.

They don't know how, or why. They just know that this will happen, and they want to play a part. They want to honor this symbol of hope, this symbol of light—this child. They want to kneel before him, before his family, on a long, dark night. They know not what else to do. But somehow, in the story, that is enough—that they believe in the hope of this child, that they believe the world can be made better, different, lovelier. Peaceful. Hopeful. Beautiful.

By this, the smallest of creatures.

Who among us, even today, wants to believe differently?

People's hearts were turned that night and have stayed turned for centuries—all because of the story of one small child being born. Because people believed that was all it took: One. Small. Child.

Savior or no, I still believe that's all it takes: the hope that one lone, helpless being can change the course of a world gone wrong, can turn hearts and minds to a better place—to making a better place. Sure, lots of people celebrate Christmas because their savior was born that night. I celebrate because a *child* was born that night, and because thousands were, and are, and will continue to be born, on that night, this night, and all the nights to follow. And with each child comes the blessed hope that things will be made right: better, peaceful, brighter. Our world can change its course, and with every night star, every birth, every gathering, that hope should be renewed. It should be recognized, acted upon, and celebrated.

Each of us, in our time, was that child. We were that hope. We *are* that hope. We perpetuate it. Each long winter's night, we are given the chance to renew that hope. If once, years ago, people stopped for even a single night in awe of the hope that one small child would make their world a better place, then perhaps we should, too. Perhaps the idea that one small, ordinary person can change our world, our lives, isn't such a crazy notion. Perhaps the thought that we can do so isn't so crazy, either.

And so, at Yule, we gather around our tiny slips of hopes and plans. We light our candles and exchange our presents. We revel in the magic and hope that is promised in the coming months. We gather with our friends and family and feast, knowing abundance is just around the corner.

Abundance. That word will lead us straight to another, more commercial element of the Christmas holiday: Santa Claus. I'm sure (in fact, I know) that his roots at some point in the distant past were much more altruistic. Somehow, through the years, Santa has increasingly become a star of the season, for followers of the original holiday as well as others. We do not leave him behind in our family, either. I confess that I get as excited about Christmas morning as the kids do. We hang the stockings, we write the letters, we make an annual pilgrimage to Macy's to meet the Man Himself.

And while we stress to Samaire and Wylie that it is as important to give as to receive, that the season is about bringing the light back into the world, there is another lesson running underneath all this that I truly treasure.

Santa is magic. Christmas morning, with its surprise and love and anticipation, is as magical as I can possibly conceive. What's even more amazing to me is that as a society—as a people—we have all silently agreed to this magic. Children will excitedly talk about Santa to whomever is closest to them at that time of year, and inevitably, the person on the other end of the conversation will smile and join in, regardless of background or belief. Astoundingly, we all, for a short period of time every year, agree that magic is important, that wonder is worth cultivating. In doing so, each of us brings into the darkness of winter the bright light of belief—belief in flying reindeer and jolly men and elves who know how to make just the right toy for every child. We go to the stores and donate toys for children whose families may have a hard time perpetuating the myth. We all, regardless of our background, virtually hold hands and bring a tangible amount of magic into the world. We protect it, guard it, and joyfully participate in it.

I see all this as a reminder that holding on to the magic of our childhood, the wonder we have for the world, is priceless and absolutely necessary. The simple deed of actively living the story, participating in the magic every year, opens my heart to recognizing so many other small moments of grace that happen around me during that time. When I am in the mode of keenly living in a wondrous story, I am more adept at seeing all the other wondrous things happening near me. I am more likely to stop and wonder at a snowfall, or feel my breath catch at a sung carol, or even feel touched by a simple "Happy holidays," because I am consciously aware of all the light and joy toward which all of us are putting our energy.

It reminds me that I should be living like that all the time. It reminds me that I should be putting forth the joy and love in my heart year-round, that regardless of what we believe, we all can create a truly magical world together when we decide to do so. All it takes is each of us deciding it can be done. I need to make that decision more often.

As a parent, and one who believes in magic truly in her heart, the idea of Santa can be bittersweet to me. I am keenly aware that the days of my children's blind belief in all things magical is on a timeline: the fairies and will-o'-the-wisps, the elves and magical beasts will not be so alive forever. I know we will cross a line at some point where my job will be to help them navigate a world where dragons and unicorns and superheroes may not exist as they see them now, and to show them that still—still—there is magic. You just have to be willing to seek it out, to recognize it when it happens, to *be* the miraculous when the world needs it.

Samaire stands on that precipice now. I see it and I desperately try to traverse it with her as painlessly as I can. I can only do so much. My heart aches as she grows old enough to see the ugliness and sadness in the world. I do what I can to show her the beauty and hope. When she was eight, her letter to Santa was different than in years past. That year, her letter explained how her friends were starting not to believe in Santa, and she wrote that it was getting harder for her to believe. "Please show me you are real," she asked. "Virginia gives me hope."

We have watched the story of Virginia and her letter to the *New York Sun* countless times. If you haven't heard of it, it's the true story of a little girl who was teased for still believing in Santa Claus. She wrote a letter to the newspaper to ask if he was real because her father told her, "If you see it in the *Sun*, it's so." The editor wrote back what is now a historically famous letter. Samaire loves the story, loves Virginia—in large part, I believe, because she feels so akin to her.

I read my girl's letter to Santa, and my heart broke. I had known this day would come, but I wasn't quite prepared. I vacillated over what to do. Sam and I had a long conversation that bled entirely too late into the night.

I decided Santa would write her a letter, a letter that would hopefully give her one last magical Christmas morning as it was and help her through the Christmases to come. I put the letter in a leather-bound notebook with a photo of Virginia at the age she was when she wrote her letter. (Thank you, oh Internet, keeper of all things.) I also carefully wrapped a copy of *The Minpins*, a book written by Samaire's favorite author, Roald Dahl. This is what the letter said:

DEAREST SAMAIRE,

This is a photo of Virginia. That photo of her was taken the year she wrote her letter to the New York Sun. If I remember correctly, and I do, she was about your age when she mailed it. I am glad you know about her, and find her an inspiration. She struggled, just like you, in believing in me—in the magic of Santa Claus. In the end, I believe she found an answer to her worries, and she lived that magic her whole life.

I very much hope you can do the same.

I know well how hard it is to believe in magic today. I wish I could make it easier on you. I wish I could promise it would always be easy after this, but I'm afraid it only gets a bit more difficult. The world often turns its eye away from the wonder that lives in it; people grow to think it's only for small children. They think magic only exists in stories of princesses and frogs and old men and flying reindeer.

I know better. Virginia did, too.

I have faith that in your heart, you know better as well.

Samaire, my dear child, magic doesn't only live in those stories. Nor does it just come from me and those like me. Magic, at its greatest, lives in you. And here's the true secret: you are one of the keepers of magic.

I can see it in the stories you write and the songs you sing. I can see it in how much you read, and how real the words on the page are to you. Not everyone is able to do those things; not everyone is able to see what you see.

And without people like you to see it, the magic in our world cannot exist.

Magic isn't just presents under trees and princely frogs, of course. It's in the smile you give a stranger, or the hug you give your daddy. It's the candy you share with Wylie, and the bread you bake with your mama. Magic exists in the love and kindness we share with each other. I exist because of the generosity abundant on Christmas night.

It is too easy to be mean and cruel in this world. It is easy to only act for ourselves, to push others aside. People turn a blind eye to their fellow humans all the time. It is normal. It is becoming increasingly expected. I find it heartbreaking. Yet, just as Virginia gives you hope, you give me hope.

Together, we can keep the magic in this world. Hold what magic is yours deep in your heart. Protect it. Witness the magic in the world around you.

Notice it. Celebrate it. Create space for it. Continue to make your magic, Samaire—write your stories, share your songs. Be recklessly kind.

I am giving you this journal to help with that. Use it to write down magical things you want to remember. Write about wonderful days you have, or moments that were dreams come true. Recognize the smallest things, and hold them close to your heart—they will build to become enormous magical paths that will only lead you to more wonderful magical moments.

That is how it happens, of course. One small act eventually grows to an enormous miracle, if only we foster it.

I started simply by giving one gift to a small, deserving child.

Dearest Samaire, hold fast. Do not waver. There is magic in this world, wonderful amazing breathtaking magic. Never hesitate to believe in it. Believe in me, but most of all . . . believe in yourself.

I believe in you.

Sincerely,
Santa Claus

P.S. I know you love Roald Dahl stories. He was a keeper of magic, too. This was his advice (hidden in the book I have left for you).

"And above all, watch with glittering eyes the whole world around you because the greatest secrets are always hidden in the most unlikely of places. Those who don't believe in magic will never find it."

—Roald Dahl, *The Minpins*

She was thrilled when she found the journal away from the other gifts, next to her pillow, wrapped in handmade paper. I hope that as the years go by, she reads the letter again and sees how much we love her and how this wasn't just about a man in a red suit but so much more.

Winter is a special time for our family. I often forget and get caught up in the running around that happens beforehand. Just when the endless parties and preparations and deadline and general chaos begin to drag me under, Yule serves as a monumental reminder to stop and concentrate on what's important. It serves as a way to remind me, when I'm fighting against the overwhelming darkness, that I have control over some of the light. Albert Camus once wrote, "In the depth of winter I finally learned that there was in me an invincible summer." It seems every Yule, this is a lesson I need to once again internalize. It is a reminder that magic is still out there sparkling in our midst, if I can dedicate myself to recognizing it, to enjoying it, to creating it with true intention.

If I were a better witch, I'd be giving you an amazing recipe for a Yule-log cake right about now. It's a traditional Yule dessert and absolutely delicious; you might better recognize it as a jelly roll cake. Unfortunately, I am not offering up the secret to this delicious confection here and now, mostly because every single time I've tried to make one they've fallen apart in a most fantastic fashion, and while I believe in making occasions as special as I can, I also believe the end of the year is hectic enough without me losing my mind trying to create a perfect jelly roll cake. You are welcome to try it, but in case you are in my camp and need something not incredibly involved, I have perfected a different delicious roll for you: the cinnamon roll. They're easy-peasy and perfect to welcome the sun as it peeks over the horizon the morning of Yule.

When I was growing up, my mom always made cinnamon rolls for us to eat after midnight mass on Christmas Eve, served with a giant cup of hot cocoa drenched in fluffy white marshmallows. I cannot recommend this pairing enough.

Cinnamon Rolls

Now, I'll be the first to admit that in a pinch I reach for the canned cinnamon rolls. You know the ones—with the little tubs of icing at the end. But while they make a very satisfying pop when you open them, they cannot compare to fresh, homemade cinnamon rolls right out of the oven. There's just something especially comforting and warm about digging a homemade roll, dripping with icing, out of a pan. Not to mention the amazing fragrance that fills your home. To me, it's a vital part of the winter holidays.

It is also especially appropriate as we welcome the light back into the world, as cinnamon is associated with the element of fire and astrologically aligned with the sun. What better spice to use as you welcome back the sun after the longest night of the year?

Cinnamon-roll recipes can seem intimidating, but hang in here with me. They are super hard to mess up; you just need to be patient with yourself and the process. (That's my own personal struggle right there.) If you take your time and relish the process, the end result is one to be savored by you and about ten of your friends. (Or, you know, just by you, ten to twelve times . . .)

DOUGH

1   cup warm milk
1   standard packet active dry yeast
⅔   cup granulated sugar
1 ½ cup unsalted butter, melted
1   teaspoon salt
1   large egg
3   cups all-purpose flour

FILLING

1   cup brown sugar
2   tablespoons ground cinnamon
     Light sprinkle of nutmeg to taste
½   cup salted butter, melted

GLAZE

4   ounces cream cheese, softened
¼   cup salted butter, softened
1   teaspoon vanilla extract
1–2 tablespoons whipping cream
2   cups powdered sugar

I always start the yeast in about half of the warm milk first, but that isn't absolutely necessary. It just makes me feel better to see it foam up; I have a constant fear that my yeast will be "broken." If you are a normal, sane person, go ahead and skip that part. Either way, find a nice large bowl and combine the milk, sugar, melted butter, salt, and egg. I like to add in about a third of the flour at this point and mix it in well, then add the yeast if it isn't already in the milk. Slowly add the rest of the flour until the dough just starts to pull away from the bowl.

More than likely, you will feel the need to add more flour. Don't. The dough should be stickier than regular bread dough but not stick completely to your hands. This assures that the rolls will be nice and soft after they bake; too much flour will ruin that. If you feel you still need to incorporate the flour better, use your hands on a lightly floured surface, but again, be careful with the use of extra flour.

Once it's nice and combined, transfer the dough to a well-greased large bowl, cover it, and let it double in size. At my house, this takes about an hour. I cook in a drafty New York City apartment with a ridiculously small kitchen that has very few places to keep the dough. Therefore, I have been known to keep my oven on Warm while I prep the dough and then turn the oven off and set the bowl inside to rise. I'm sure this is against some sort of cooking or baking rule somewhere, but so far it's worked out well for me.

Toward the end of the hour, combine your sugar, cinnamon, and nutmeg for the filling in a small bowl. I always make a bit extra (okay, I've been known to double the measurements), as I love a roll exploding with filling. It makes it a little messy, but so delicious.

Once the dough has doubled, you'll need to get ready to take it out and start to assemble it into rolls. This part is key for me—most recipes here will tell you to lightly flour a large surface and roll out the dough. I, however, have no such large surface available. So I like to take the absolute largest baking sheet I own, grease it with butter, and dump the dough onto that. I then push down the dough to the edges of the pan. You can use your hands, or if you're fancy and own a rolling pin, I hear those work well, too.

Once the dough is rolled out, brush it with the melted butter for the filling. Don't hold back; this is one of the deliciousness factors. Then liberally spread the filling across the dough, all the way to the edges. This is where the baking pan serves its purpose, as you can get right up to the edge of the dough without a big mess.

Now, this is where I do something a bit odd: I spray my hands with cooking spray. It keeps them from sticking too much to the dough at first as I tightly roll it up, moving from the edge closest to me outward. You should end up with a nice long roll of dough filled with cinnamon. At this point, take a moment and relish the fact you've gotten this far. I always do. I might actually also call over family members to admire our short-lived Yule log—that is, if I managed to not tear a bunch of holes in the dough due to impatience. Slow and steady, friends, when making that roll. It makes all the difference.

I like to bake the rolls in round pans. Before I begin to cut the dough into smaller rolls, I prep the pan by greasing it with butter (again!!) and lightly sprinkling it with a bit of the extra filling, or just plain sugar if you don't have extra filling (if this is the case, good for you!).

I admit I'm full of strange ideas in this recipe, and I am not about to stop now. In order to get the cleanest cut from this long roll, you are going to want to use dental floss. That's right, the kind that you clean your teeth with—but, pro tip, *not* the mint flavor. That will ruin these rolls quicker than anything; take my word for it. Slide a length of floss under the roll about 2 inches from the end and then pull it up as if you are getting ready to tie it. It should slide through the dough smoothly.

Place the rolls in the pans and once again let them rise for about 30 minutes in a warm space. After about 20 minutes, I like to preheat my oven to 350 degrees Fahrenheit. The rolls will get nice and puffy, and that's when you know it's time to bake them. Place them in the oven for about 15–20 minutes.

While they cook, mix together your icing. Start with the softened cream cheese, butter, vanilla, and whipping cream. Once those ingredients are nicely combined, slowly add in your powdered sugar. I like my icing a bit thicker and fluffy, but if you prefer more of a glaze, use less sugar and more cream. Mess with the proportions until they're just right for you.

When the rolls are finished, I like to put a portion of the icing on right away and let it melt all over the top. Once they are cool enough to eat, I add another dollop of icing and a sprinkling of cinnamon.

Now grab your mug of hot chocolate and welcome the sun in style!

Cinnamon is one excellent filling, but you can add a number of fillings to these rolls. I prefer cinnamon for its special meaning, on top of my affinity for its taste, but any of the following might appeal to you more; I suggest trying all of them and seeing what's best for you. This recipe can be repurposed for many of the holidays throughout the year and doesn't have to stand in for a Yule log. Experiment with the ingredients below, as well as any others that might sound delicious, and create your own special recipes and traditions.

Pumpkin: Pumpkin is associated with the moon goddess and is often symbolic of protection, love, fertility, and prosperity. Filling the rolls with pumpkin puree and a sprinkling of maple syrup and topping them with walnuts makes them the essence of fall in a delicious bundle, a wonderful Samhain dessert.

Honey: Honey was said to be the food of the gods in ancient Greece and has been revered across cultures and throughout history for its healing properties. In Jewish tradition, honey is eaten at the arrival of the new year to bring sweetness in the coming times. Making this recipe into honey buns is super simple: just spread honey on the dough instead of the cinnamon mixture, then drizzle more honey along the top when they are taken out of the oven. (You could also add walnuts to the filling if you'd like a bit of crunch.)

Jam: Strawberries symbolize spring and rebirth. They are closely linked with friendship and love. Spread strawberry jam on the dough as the filling to add a special bit of love and hope to your rolls. Topping the rolls with a light lemon glaze could make for a wonderfully bright treat for Ostara, the spring equinox.

IMBOLC

Imbolc (pronounced *i-molg*) is when the promise of Yule begins to feel fulfilled. It is near this day when the light, which has been inching in minute by minute, finally reaches a point where our days are starting to feel longer. Our mornings are a bit brighter, our evenings a bit slower. Imbolc lands halfway between the winter solstice (Yule) and the spring equinox (Ostara) and marks the beginning of spring.

Imbolc falls traditionally during lambing season, when the natural world seems bursting with the promise of new life. Crocuses and daffodils begin to push through the snow; the prospect of surviving the long cold season begins to feel real. Imbolc is full of hope and anticipation. There is an underlying energy of expectation that permeates this time of year. Potential lies just below the surface; roots are growing and leaves are just beginning to reach above the earth. We finally leave the darkness behind and step into the growing sun. Imbolc is the promise that better times are coming. It is a time to make room for growth and renewal, to clear space in our homes and our hearts for the sacred and the enduring possibility of every spring.

Imbolc is tied to the festival of the goddess Brigid, known also by Brigit, Brighid, and a number of other variations on the name. She is the goddess of inspiration, fertility, fire, and water. She is closely associated with home and hearth, as well as poetry and the healing arts. She symbolizes the elements needed to spark growth (fertility, fire, water, sun, and warmth) and what is needed to nurture that growth (home and hearth, as well as healing). She is the spark of creativity: creation itself.

The traditions around honoring Brigid are many, ranging from setting out food and drink and making a bed for her so she might enter and bless your home, to setting bonfires that are kept burning for days to honor her. Small dolls representing her are made of straw to bring fertility and good fortune; what are known as "Brigid's crosses" are folded from long rushes to be displayed by a home's hearth as a sign of protection.

Brigid is said to protect homes and livestock, to keep the fires burning through the last of the winter and bring prosperity to the coming months. Brigid guides the earth back to abundance, planting the seeds that will lead to the renewal of life found in the onset of longer, warmer days.

Brigid was the initial spark of spring and greatly revered in Gaelic traditions—so greatly, in fact, that as Christianity spread across Ireland and Scotland, the newly converted Gaels managed to win her canonization as a saint. She continued to be so beloved by her followers that she became known as "the Mary of the Gael." To this day, St. Brigid's feast day coincides with the timing of Imbolc.

Brigid gets special favor at our house, in fact, for one of her deeds as a saint, funnily enough. Ever the healer, she went to care for a leper colony, only to find they had no beer to drink. Through the sheer strength of her blessing, she turned their bathwater into beer to nourish them—no small miracle. Sam leads a special toast in her honor every Imbolc.

Imbolc doesn't often share the level of ceremony or prominence on the Wheel of the Year accorded to any of the solstices or equinoxes. As a cross-quarter day, it lies quietly after Yule, whispering the promise of better things to come. Just as the earth gradually shakes off the snow and harsh cold of winter and the light seeps slowly into our days, Imbolc gently reminds us that there is hope forever underlying whatever we may face. We need only make room for it.

Making room is a tradition I follow during this time of year, unmistakably: room for new beginnings both in my heart and in my physical space. Imbolc is a brilliant time to clear your mind and heart for new adventures, to allow for inspiration to guide you. It is a time to let go of what's not working, to release the fear or reluctance that is holding you back and give yourself permission to take a chance, make a plan, grow in a direction you haven't explored.

This opportunity can come in many forms. Imbolc is an excellent time to start a new habit, to let it grow as the world around you grows. It's a time to begin writing the book you always wanted to write or to take a class on something you always wanted to learn. Imbolc reminds us that we are renewed just as the world is renewed, and that there is constant hope to improve our lives and bring them closer to the stories we wish to make real.

For me to begin anything new, I have to have a clear space to do so—not just a mind clear of a million chores or of fear and nervousness, but an actual clear space. Spring cleaning falls during this time for a reason. After being cooped up inside for months on end, now is the time to throw open the windows and breathe the crisp air. Now is when I take to my closet and clear it of the clothes I no longer wear, when I inch my way across our tiny apartment playing my never-ending game of Jenga organization, attempting to free up just a few more square feet. I get rid of the things we have held on to that we don't really need. I audit what we've kept of the kids' schoolwork and choose the truly memorable and significant pieces to put away for posterity. We go through toys that are no longer played with, books no longer read, clothes that have long since become too small, and package them up to be donated and used where they can be truly appreciated.

I scrub our bathroom and kitchen. I vacuum and dust. I slowly think of the past months and intentionally push out all the things I no longer want in our space. I burn sage. I light candles and buy air fresheners that remind us of the spring to come and make our home a place that feels open and clean and ready for a new beginning.

It's amazing the effect it has on me mentally when my physical space is clean and open. I feel like it gives my ever-running mind some space to truly think. It's as if creating a clear, open physical space somehow unlocks the same inside my heart and mind. I can't create something new inside myself if my physical self feels crowded and overwhelmed. Paying attention to our home and the kind of space we need to flourish in provides us all with the mental space to do that flourishing.

Often, the kids and I will buy small seeds to plant and set on our windowsill, so we can watch close-up the miracle of spring emerging from the winter. We go to the community garden and help clear out the remnants of the past months so the new plants have room to mature. We count the birds on our walks through our neighborhood as they slowly begin to once again fill the trees.

Imbolc is a time to light candles and remember that warmth and rebirth is just around the corner. It's also a time to remember that it's up to us to create the space that can allow the promised renewal to happen. We must let go and move forward, trusting that what lies ahead is infinitely better than what is behind—trusting that we can make it so.

I love this time of year. I love the idea of the potential of creation simmering just below the surface, waiting for just the right time to come to full fruition.

This time of year seems the perfect time to create a sweet promise for those you love. Bananas align with the symbolism that surrounds Brigid in that they are often used to promote fertility and prosperity, so banana bread, with its sweet smell of the coming summer, is the perfect treat for Imbolc.

A few years ago, my daughter decided she wanted to learn how to make the perfect banana bread for her father, and we spent weeks making it over and over again to get it right. Now, every spring, we pull out our recipe and bake that bread once again. As it's a recipe made by and for a child, the measurements are pretty loose. The main goal is to pour as much excitement about adventures yet to come and love of the person you will share them with into the making.

Samaire and Daddy's Golden Banana Bread

Baking spray
⅓ cup unsalted butter
6 medium-sized bananas
1 egg
¾ cup granulated sugar
1 teaspoon vanilla
1 teaspoon baking soda
Salt
1 ½ cups all-purpose flour
Butterscotch chips
½ cup brown sugar
2 more bananas, thinly sliced

Preheat the oven to 350 degrees Fahrenheit.

Melt the butter in a small bowl. We usually microwave it for about 20–30 seconds; it doesn't need to be completely melted. Peel and slice the six bananas. This is an excellent task for small hands, as the bananas don't require sharp knives and these six don't need to be perfectly, or even neatly, sliced.

Once the bananas are sliced, put them in a medium-sized bowl and mash. The bananas should no longer be solid, but a little chunky in spots is good. Next, pour in the butter. Since I often have small people making this recipe with me, we crack the egg into a separate small bowl and beat it with a fork before adding it into the banana-and-butter mixture. Stir until combined well. This can easily be done with a regular spoon or fork.

Once your mixture is nicely combined, add in the sugar and vanilla. Mix well, and then add in the baking soda and a pinch of salt. Add in the flour about half a cup at a time, slowly stirring to blend. Add butterscotch chips to taste. (I try to keep it to two child's handfuls.) Same with the brown sugar—you can measure it out, but it's usually also two little hands full. Stir the chips and sugar into the batter.

Spray a 4 × 8" loaf pan with the baking spray to keep the batter from sticking. Pour the batter into the loaf pan and then top with the sliced bananas. (We like to make flower patterns with them along the top of the loaf.) Cook the bread for one hour. Serve to Daddy with a big smile on your face.

Ostara, or Eostera (Spring Equinox)

Ostara (O-*stahr*-uh), the first day of spring, inevitably arrives cold despite the teasing of the days and weeks before. Nonetheless, it heralds the fact that winter is over and warmth and light have officially returned. Ostara stands on the edge of that return, balancing light with dark and reminding us that the time of growth and reflection is over and the time for renewal and action has come. As the earth awakes, so shall we. It is time to bring what has started as mere roots into the coming sun.

Ostara often falls very near Easter, and while I found it hard to leave behind the stories and traditions of Christmas, it was much easier for me to let go of a lot of the Easter mythology. The overlapping theme of rebirth is absolutely undeniable, but the journey there is vastly different. As I grow older and less inclined to the dramatic, the story of someone needing to be tortured to save my soul, willingly or not, is one I am relieved not to pass on to my children. They know the story, and every year when they ask I once again repeat it, always beginning with "Remember the baby they celebrate at Christmas . . ." and then cringe a bit inside as I tell the tale.

This is not to say I do anything to dishonor it; in fact, I always try to impart the amazing selflessness of Jesus's sacrifice and encourage them to think about how it must feel to believe someone was willing to give up so much on behalf of you and others. I just also well remember the guilt I felt on Good Friday, sitting in a church that was dark, silent, and filled with overwhelming grief. I can easily recall the heaviness my heart felt, not fully understanding why Jesus had to be so tortured, what we might do again to cause such an awful thing to have to be done. I am relieved I can avoid sharing those same feelings with my children.

However, while we don't believe our savior rises from the dead, we do honor the hope that accompanies the natural awakening that comes with spring: the renewal of the world that surrounds us, the promise of abundant light and energy and joy. I remember well the dawn chorus on Easter morning as a child, the delight that radiated through the parishioners after the quiet, dark, and sorrow-ridden previous days. It seemed everyone in our community took a collective thankful breath. The day was lighter, the energy palpably different. We wore bright colors and dressed in our best clothes. The feeling of sheer happiness and celebration was undeniable, that feeling all the more precious for the dichotomy of the previous days.

I try to bring my children that same sense of joy as we go outside and recognize the earth on the precipice of creation, of creating. Their grandparents routinely call with news of calves at that time of year. Our walks in Central Park fill with tiny, newly born birds; our zoo explorations burst with paper announcements on the enclosure windows announcing the arrivals of small creatures.

We rejoice in the shoots pushing up through the soil in our garden, the tulips now flooding the pathways with their brightly colored buds. The last of the snow is melting, and a warmer wind prevails. Sam and the kids and I start to dream of what our garden will be this year, we count the buds now present on our giant magnolia tree. We rejoice in a world bursting with life and activity. There is a feeling here, a tangible energy in our city, when the weather lifts and suddenly our doors are flung open. It's a shared joyous celebration that percolates and rushes out in crowds to the streetside tables of restaurants and the open parks and greenways, a feeling that as a community we all are breathing a collective sigh of relief that, at long last, winter is over. You see it in the smiles and welcoming hugs of neighbors who have been missed in the colder months, of children yelling and running through the now-packed playgrounds. In the bodegas, doors are flung open and music spills out onto the sidewalk.

It is an unbelievably special and precious time, standing on the precipice of what feels like only brighter things to come.

On Ostara—a moment of equal day and night, light and dark, warm and cold—we pause to look behind us at what we have nurtured in the months previously and what we can help flourish in the months to come. Ostara acts as a gateway, a door to step through with all the plans and dreams and hopes we whispered in the quiet dark of winter. It's a call to bring it all to light, a call to bring intention to our actions and make what was once just ponderings actuality. It is a celebration of the moment before light overcomes the dark, the intake of breath before the furor of activity.

At our house, like many others, this involves painting eggs. I tell my children a tale of a small garden readying itself for the return of the spring goddess: how the flowers put on their best colors and the shoots of grass struggled through the snow to give her a soft place to walk, how the trees burst forth in leaves and blooms and the birds readied their chicks to sing.

I tell them there was a rabbit who, watching all this preparation, felt he had nothing to give. He sat alone in the middle of the garden, unable to find a way to contribute to this welcoming of a long-missed maiden. The garden paused, not knowing how to help the little bunny. Then a mama robin hopped from her nest and offered the bunny the pieces of blue eggshell from which her small brood was born. She carefully brought him each and every piece, no matter how small, in hopes he could find a way to give the goddess his own special gift.

And so the bunny sat and moved the pieces this way and that. Slowly, he decided what to do, and then carefully, ever so carefully, he managed to put together the pieces to form a few small, hollow eggs. Worried over the cracks and rough edges, he borrowed colors from the grass and flowers and painted over them. He painted his hopes and dreams for the coming months, beautiful flowers and hopeful words. He painstakingly recreated the beauty of his flower friends and the determination of the small birds just earning their wings.

When he was done, he looked down and still saw not enough. All he could see were broken pieces barely held together and brushes of paint haphazardly run across them. He hid them in shame and then hid himself with them.

But his friends in the garden saw something different. They recognized the beauty of what he'd made. When the goddess arrived, oohing and ahhing over the flowers and birds, they did what they could to lead her to the hidden eggs. The flowers bent toward the smallest of them, hidden deep in their stalks. The tree crowned the ones hidden amongst its roots. Soon the goddess had an armful of the fragile painted eggs.

She sat down and asked for the rabbit. "Come here," she whispered. "You've nothing to fear."

The rabbit hopped slowly from his burrow, cheeks burning in embarrassment. He was sure the garden had made fun of him, sure the goddess would be nothing but disappointed in him.

But she was not.

She praised his painting, she lauded his careful work, she cried tears of joy over the hopes he shared, over small cracks and broken shell. Soon the bunny was sitting up with pride. The garden was not making fun of him, and the goddess was not disappointed. She told the bunny she would look forward every year to finding small eggs painted with hopes throughout the garden. And so every year, the bunny paints his small eggs, hiding them throughout the garden for the goddess to find.

We, too, paint our little eggs to hide and find. We sit over cups of dye and crayons and wax and talk of what we hope the warmer months will bring, what we will bring to the coming months. We discuss the beauty we can contribute to the world if we act with intention, if we care enough to pause and bring our best to even the smallest task. We discuss how lucky we are to have a day to pause and appreciate the turn of the season. We remember how lucky we were to have months where we could curl up indoors with each other and learn new things and plan new adventures, and how lucky we are to have months ahead of us to make them all real.

My Ostara, my first day of spring, might not be about resurrection anymore, but it is still about renewal. I breathe deep and write down my hopes. I appreciate, deeply, the moment in time I have to reflect and anticipate.

Our meals on Ostara reflect that anticipation of light and the enjoyment of all that's to come. We make deviled eggs to welcome back the sun, small orbs of yellow warmed with paprika. And I always make a big pot of springtime risotto, filled with the bright yellows and greens awaiting us just around the corner.

SPRINGTIME RISOTTO

1   pound pancetta, diced
2   bundles (approximately 2 pounds) asparagus
3   cloves garlic
5   cups low-salt chicken broth
2   tablespoons olive oil
½   cup chopped yellow onion
1 ½ cups Arborio rice
½   cup dry white wine
2   tablespoons tumeric
4   tablespoons butter
    Freshly grated Parmesan cheese (about 3 ounces)

Fry the diced pancetta in a saucepan until crispy. Set aside on a paper towel.

Take half the asparagus and break off the top halves into sections. Place onto a baking sheet and toss in olive oil and generous amounts of salt and pepper. Roast in the oven at 400 degrees Fahrenheit for approximately 30 minutes or until crisp.

Chop up the other stalks of asparagus (top halves only) and mince garlic. Throw both asparagus and garlic into lightly salted boiling water for about 3 minutes. Drain and then add asparagus into a pitcher blender with just enough water to blend. Blend until reasonably smooth.

Heat the chicken broth in a small saucepan, just short of boiling, then turn down the heat to low to keep it warm. Pour olive oil into a heavy pot and heat just to steaming. Put in the onions and let them soften for about 5 minutes. Then add the rice. Toast the rice for another couple minutes and then add in the wine. Stir until the wine is fully absorbed. Keep stirring and cooking; the mixture should start to appear creamy. Once this happens, begin to add the chicken broth, one ladleful at a time. Keep stirring and add in more broth as the previous ladleful is absorbed. Continue until all the broth has been added, still stirring. (Man, the stirring! It's worth it, though; I promise!) You will be adding in broth and stirring for approximately 20 minutes.

Once 20 minutes have passed, add in the asparagus puree. Stir until it is well incorporated. Add in two teaspoons of turmeric (this will impart a warm flavor as well as a lovely yellow color).

Remove from heat and add in the butter. Stir in the butter until it melts into the risotto.

Top each serving with roasted asparagus, diced pancetta, and Parmesan cheese. Eat at a table filled with tulips and beautifully painted eggs.

Beltane

Beltane ("*Bell*-tinn-uh") falls halfway between the spring equinox and the summer solstice. It sits opposite Samhain on the great wheel of the year and in turn holds an almost opposite honorific. Where Samhain is in between and honors those who have come before, Beltane is the assurance of the present and all that the future promises.

Beltane celebrates the union of the god and goddess, the sacred marriage of two opposing forces brought together in partnership and love. It is a festival of unity, when the anticipation of spring has been fulfilled. It is a time to honor the god and goddess, man and woman. The promise and fulfillment of creation abounds with the first showing of crops in the fields and the increase of livestock from the spring. Beltane is a time to celebrate not the first flush of love but the deeper, enduring promise of it.

Beltane has in its roots all that those who perpetuate witchy stereotypes hope for—it is often viewed from the outside as a near-orgy centering on sex and abundance. Through the ages, it has often been celebrated as such, across history and cultures, a pagan ritual flush with primal urges and feral abandonment.

Wicca finds no shame or sin in the act of sex; it is powerful and powerfully symbolic. The unity of the god and goddess, the combining of intention and divine power, is seen as sacred. Finding and experiencing that power is not just accepted but encouraged. But in truth, while Wicca honors the true pleasure and power in sex, the union of the male and female, Beltane is absolutely about so much more.

Beltane is a time for celebrating all kinds of unions—when two or more separate things join together to form a new and more complete whole. Beltane is a time of joy and revelation in who we are and who we become when we unite together in all the ways that doing so is possible. It is a time to celebrate the people in our lives who see and support us for who we are, the people around us who help make us *us*. It is a time to reconnect, to revisit and renew our relationships with those we love on all levels, to honor the strength that comes not from joining another person to make a whole but wholly loving someone as a separate being. The difference is a razor's edge, and Beltane challenges us to live that difference. It is in that difference that we can accept the dichotomy that comes with relationships that challenge us, that make us better.

One of the first times I met Sam, he was sprawled along the length of a friend's couch, hands behind his head and feet up on the armrest while I glowered at him, arms crossed, leaning against the opposite wall.

Somehow, we got into a debate about war and violence. My hippie art-school spirit held tightly to the ideology that violence couldn't solve anything; truly, it could only perpetuate an existing problem. His journalism major and history minor had left him with an entirely different point of view. I don't really remember the details of the conversation, but what I do remember was that neither of us would back down. Both of us had valid points, and we sparred relentlessly.

We only paused an hour in, when my friend Leslie came up from the basement. "It's going to be hours before they decide what we're all doing tonight. Is it always this difficult?"

I turned from my new nemesis to address her concern, which was valid.

The discussion of where we would all go next had been going on for quite some time. This wasn't new; our mutual friends regularly took longer than most people would deem necessary to put forth a united plan of action. We were in a town that rarely offered more than two or three options after ten o'clock on a Sunday night. But our friends were nice people and wanted to all agree, so the conversation sputtered on and on and on.

I decided to play my ace. "You, Leslie, obviously have arrived unprepared." I pulled a full bottle of Grey Goose from my purse with the requisite flourish, earning a bright smile from my comrade-in-arms. As she turned to get glasses from the cupboards, she nodded toward the couch. "I see you've been conversing with my brother. Did you even get her name before haranguing her, Sam?"

He smiled as he disengaged himself from the couch, spitting, "She's a pacifist!" from across the room.

"He's a warmonger," I growled. Then I handed him a shot of vodka.

Thus we started the dance that would eventually find us woven unabashedly together for Beltanes to come.

We had fits and starts in the beginning. I'd like to say this meet-cute story was part of a wonderfully structured romantic comedy, ending in birds flying out the cathedral doors as we danced down the steps. Yet we all know by now that didn't happen. What did happen is that months went by, perhaps a whole year, before I saw or spoke to him again.

All I knew after that vodka toast was that he was someone I couldn't easily forget. Sam was all confidence. He was sure of himself—not just sure of but *comfortable* with himself—and I had learned that was incredibly hard to find. Sam was the kind of person I could debate with for hours, because he wasn't going to get upset that I disagreed. In fact, he reveled in it. I loved the fact we could ardently come from different sides and stay there a while.

Then stop. Move on. Find other things.

Sam was unapologetically himself, and to someone who had been working assiduously at defining her own being, he was pretty intoxicating—and downright infuriating. He was my polar opposite in so many ways, yet we connected on all the levels that matter. To this day, you can bet we will lock horns on any number of topics. He pushes me to be thoughtful, he refuses to let me be anything other than my biggest and best self. He challenges me. He makes me better. Our lives have twined together to create something new and wonderful; we stand united despite all our differences. I believe we can stand united *because of* our differences. I would not be who I am without Sam in my life. He loves me for who I am, all on my own.

That kind of polarity and unification is what Beltane celebrates: the idea that two separate and different energies can come together to form an entirely new, better creation without compromising what made them unique to begin with. Due to that significant demarcation, a lot of the traditions of Beltane involve weaving items, the coming together of separate things into symbolic, sacred unions to create a more balanced whole: the interlacing of flowers and ribbons into crowns, the plaiting of hair, the weaving of paper to create baskets, and the famous maypole's intertwined ribbons.

Every year in our community garden we have a Beltane celebration. A maypole is erected and people gather to dance around it. It's never put forth as a pagan celebration, and Wicca is never outright mentioned, yet it is the closest I get to falling into a traditional witchy role. Every year I look forward to the festivities. We go down to the grape arbor and weave flower crowns, then, accompanied by local musicians, we dance around the pole, intricately weaving colorful ribbons into a striking design. The symbolism of the maypole is pretty blatant: the pole represents the god, the ribbons the goddess. The final outcome is the beauty they create together.

I predictably lose my place as I crouch and jump over and around the other dancers. Samaire and Wylie, one of them almost always holding my hand, will inevitably get tangled among the other participants. Yet there in our small garden, with magnolia blossoms falling on our heads and slightly off-key music playing in the background, we find one another. We clasp our hands together and laugh. We three fall to the ground, into the soft new grass, and joyously welcome the new season, while Sam usually stands off to the side, camera in hand, crooked flower crown over his ball cap.

Beltane reminds us we are a "we."

Beltane reminds us that this fact is worth celebrating with every fiber of our being.

Our present is a gift. The life we have built is worth cherishing, and our greatest act should be remaining truly connected to all of it. On Beltane, I like to remember the gift of that connection, the gift of the love of fairy tales and living dreams. I know well I live a blessed life, and Beltane serves as a reminder for me to cherish that.

My aunt Judy had a recipe that serves just such a purpose. She lived a life with her great love, my uncle Phil, and never was there a time when I couldn't palpably feel their connection when I was with them. Judy and Phil were reminders of a love that could last—of the possibility of two souls somehow weaving together a life and love that could stand the test of time. And so, I offer you her shrimp étouffée recipe: a little spicy, a lot delicious. Make it with love in your heart and those you cherish will feel it, I promise.

Étouffée literally means "smothered." May you and the ones you love be absolutely smothered in everything wonderful this glorious Beltane.

Judy's Shrimp Étouffée

2   sticks of butter
1 ½ cups chopped onions
1 ½ cups chopped celery
    Tabasco sauce to taste
4   tablespoons paprika
5   tablespoons all-purpose flour
2   tablespoons cornstarch
3   10-ounce cans of chicken stock
2   pounds crawfish (cooked and peeled) or shrimp
    Cajun seasoning (see my recipe below if you don't have a mix on hand)
⅓   cup chopped green onion tops

Put the butter in a large sauté pan. Add in the onions and celery (we sub-stitute green peppers in my house, as Sam hates celery) and cook until the vegetables are soft. Add Tabasco (I find this is *totally* a matter of taste, and if you're nervous about how much to include, you can hold off until the end and add it over the cooked dish. For me it's a solid teaspoon, two if I'm feeling sassy.) and paprika.

Add in flour and cornstarch in batches until combined well, stirring constantly. The mixture will be thick and clumpy. Add chicken stock a cup at a time and simmer for 20 minutes. Once nice and simmered, add in the crawfish tails or shrimp (or both!), green onion tops, and Cajun seasoning to taste.

I like to toss my shrimp lightly in some extra seasoning and grill with a touch of butter first so they're nice and crisp, but cook them however you find most tasty. Simmer another 15 minutes. Serve over cooked rice or quinoa. If you want to get really fancy, pour each serving of étouffée into a shallow bowl, then pack the rice or quinoa in a quarter cup or half cup measuring cup. Turn the cup carefully over the center of the bowl to get a nice stack of rice in the middle of your étouffée.

At my house, we often use Tony Chachere's Creole seasoning, and my cousin Kathy (Aunt Judy's oldest daughter) offered up one called Slap Ya Mama, which I wish I had on hand simply for the name. However, if you can't find a Cajun or Creole seasoning where you are, or you simply forgot to get it at the store, the ingredients below will work in a pinch. A small tip: while the terms "Creole seasoning" and "Cajun seasoning" are often used interchangeably, they are often *not* quite the same. Creole tends to be a bit sweeter and mild. Cajun often contains paprika, which adds to its warmth, so when searching for it at the store, keep that in mind.

3   tablespoons kosher or sea salt

3   tablespoons paprika (sweet is my recommendation)

2   tablespoons garlic powder

2   tablespoons onion powder

1   tablespoon dried thyme

1   tablespoon black pepper

2   teaspoons cayenne pepper

This seasoning is also great for use on just about anything, so if I make it at home I will often double the recipe, as we tend to go through it pretty quickly. If your family isn't as seasoning-happy as mine, store it in a cool dark place and it should be good for six months. Enjoy!

LITHA (SUMMER SOLSTICE)

I celebrated Litha (*Lee*-thah), the summer solstice, long before I became Wiccan. There was something that spoke to me about the longest day of the year, about reveling in the day of greatest light before night slowly increased, inch by inch. Of course, this day falls right smack in the middle of the summer, a time already filled with celebration. When I was a child, it was in the center of the second most-anticipated time of year: summer break. As I got older, it increasingly signified freedom and independence, summer jobs and music-festival road trips.

In college, I looked forward to knowing I could always come home to the friends I had grown up with. Summer was about reunions. The small circle of friends with whom I had endured some of the most formative moments of my life so far had spread to the winds when it came time to seek out our dreams and the higher education to get us there. Summer seemed to be one of the few times I could be certain to find myself standing in a park with them all around me, or sitting in a coffee shop for hours, sneaking rum into my mocha and listening to them play and sing. It was my version of heaven. To this day, when we are all together, a part of me shines with happiness that most days I forget is even there.

Knowing our time in summer was fleeting, between jobs and camps and school and everything else, made it precious. We squeezed every hour out of the day and most of the night. So long before I recognized Litha itself, I was celebrating the solstice. It felt like a turning point in our summer, a signifier that our time was running down, and I always wanted to pause and relish what we had right then. I wanted to do something, anything, that day and night. I wanted us to pause for a moment before we once again ran out into the world. I knew in my heart these summers themselves were already running down in number, that we had precious few left before we would all be working and not getting months off during the warmest part of the year to revel.

Our first summer back from college, the first one where we had all left and come back, most of us were working over the solstice. A group of my friends had left weeks before, to jobs far away, and the rest of us were simply resting in Salina before we were off to other things. It was the first time we didn't have three whole months to concoct horrendous mixtures of candy and nacho cheese at the public pool, or jump in a car to head to whatever music festival or concert struck our fancy.

I was a bit down, and my friend Scott shared both my restlessness at the absence of what had always felt like an enduring reality and a willingness to recognize this moment in the year. So we jumped in my small red Geo Metro convertible and spent the afternoon into the evening doing whatever came to mind in our small town, with whomever we could find available. We put the top down and sang too loudly with the stereo. We drove too fast, we laughed too much. We climbed to the top of Coronado Heights (what can only be termed a hill, but still a notable one, in the middle of the Kansas Plains) and surveyed all that lay before us. We drank in our home and its endlessness. We pushed its small boundaries and enjoyed its familiar minutiae. We lived that day, every hour of it. When it was finally time to call it, we sat in Scott's driveway with the seats laid back, looking at the stars, reminiscing about all that had come before and speculating about all that lay ahead of us.

That first year away had made our paths to our dreams very real. He and I both had callings in our hearts that felt like there was nothing else we could do but follow them to the end, wherever that might take us. We had both chosen, had been lucky enough to have been chosen, to go to schools that challenged and pushed us. It had been an exhausting and wonderful and terrifying and amazingly hopeful year.

Sitting there in Scott's all but silent neighborhood, we talked through that year and what the next held as the stars turned over us. We talked about how much we wanted the other to succeed. We talked about how frightening both succeeding and failing could be. I gave him a small book I had made at school. It wasn't much, but I wanted him to know that though we were time zones apart, I still held him in my heart. I was still thinking of him, rooting for him, just as I knew he was rooting for me.

"Happy solstice."

Scott held it to his chest and then said, "I have a gift for you, too."

With that, he got out of the car to stand there before my headlights. I climbed out of the driver's seat and slid onto the hood of my car and there, on what has now become my favorite stage in all the world, there on the cracked concrete of his driveway in front of his garage door, bathed in the low lights of my Metro, Scott began to sing.

I wish I could tell you what it was he sang, but I can't. I can tell you it was Italian and that while I didn't understand a word of it, it spoke to me still. There, in the middle of our small town in the middle of our flyover state in the middle of our vast country, my soul was renewed. His voice carried up over me and my car and our minuscule lives and seemed to rise to the stars themselves. It reminded me that even though our days together were numbered, even though the light of summer was quickly passing, the darkness that was coming wasn't about sadness or loss or despair. It was about growth and learning and looking into ourselves. It was about going where we needed to go so we could do just this: bring our gifts out into the light when it was time.

The increasing darkness wasn't about preparing for loss. It was about preparing for growth.

I didn't know, sitting on the hood of my car that night, that I was learning a lesson about a holiday I would celebrate with my children decades later. I didn't know that I had just discovered the true meaning of the summer solstice, the meaning I would carry with me the rest of my life. I missed the moment then, but looking back, I know that is exactly what happened that night. I feel it now with as much fervor as I did then, watching my friend sing beneath the stars and move my heart in a way that I hadn't expected. I remember thinking in that moment that yes, *this* was why we had run forward, why we had run toward those places that tried every part of us. Why we had run toward our dreams and where they might lead us. All the loneliness I had felt without my friends, all the fear of success or failure, all the doubt that I had left too much behind, slowly faded away. I learned to look forward to the darkness edging into my days.

Litha is about celebrating every second of the sun and all it gives us as much as it is about preparing our hearts for the time of growth and reflection ahead. Litha is about treasuring what's around us and understanding that it is fleeting. It reminds us to celebrate as we move along the wheel of life. Litha is a time to renew your commitments, to promise that you are dedicated to what and whom you love in times of abundance as well as in the times of quiet to come. Sam and I renewed our vows last solstice, as the sun set over the Mediterranean Sea, promising to stand by each other no matter the length of days or nights to come. As we stood on Midsummer, in the retreating light of the day, a lot had passed between us in the years since we last made these promises. We knew what it was like to walk in a frightening darkness that was ever increasing and what it meant to truly be each other's light. Our vows that evening surged with true understanding of what it meant to live under a dying sun and not fear any darkness that might come. Darkness is not diminishing but empowering. A key element of Midsummer is abundance—abundance of crops, of light, of love. Summer solstice is when I often look at my life and try to fully recognize the sheer amount of joy and blessings around me, to take nothing for granted. Sam and I knew we had been blessed with abundance, standing as we did in one of the most beautiful places in the world, our healthy, happy children in our arms and three of our most precious family members by our sides.

Midsummer is about recognizing that light in our lives, the abundance it brings. It reminds us of what can happen when we share nurturing and loving energy. We celebrate and revel in that energy on Litha and we remind ourselves that the light that exists is only possible because of the darkness that gives us time to reflect and cultivate.

Our Litha is filled with flowers and the harvest from our small garden. We make foods that celebrate the summer—bright colors, fresh flavors, and decadent desserts. We spoil ourselves at Midsummer; we swim in the abundance of our lives. We appreciate it. We celebrate it.

In the midst of our barbecued and honeyed meats and corn salads and bright, fresh vegetables, I like to make a dessert to remind us that the darkness to come is worth relishing, too. When I was growing up, my mom always made me chocolate pudding cake for special occasions. It was her mother's recipe, and I adore it. It is dark and decadent and perfect to remind us that the coming night is something to be celebrated.

CHOCOLATE PUDDING CAKE

1	cup flour
¾	cup sugar
2	tablespoons cocoa
2	tablespoons baking powder
¼	teaspoon salt
½	cup milk
2	tablespoons shortening, melted (or butter if you don't have shortening)
1	cup brown sugar, packed
⅓	cup cocoa
1 ⅓ cups hot water	

Preheat your oven to 350 degrees Fahrenheit. In a large mixing bowl, combine the flour, sugar, 2 tablespoons cocoa, baking powder, and salt. Slowly stir in milk and shortening (or butter). Pour this batter into a square 9 x 9" baking pan.

Stir the brown sugar and the rest of the cocoa together in a separate bowl until well combined. Sprinkle over the cake batter.

I like to place the baking pan on a shelf in the oven, then pour the hot water evenly over the ingredients in the pan. Close the oven and bake for 45 minutes. Wonderfully, there's no need to wait when it's out of the oven, you can go ahead and serve it hot. Cut into squares and invert onto the dessert plate. Make sure to spoon the extra sauce over the cake.

You can also wait for it to cool and serve it cold; I just am never quite able to make it that far. Once, when I was pregnant with Samaire, I made this cake for Midsummer and ended up eating the whole pan myself with a spoon, straight out of the baking dish—not my proudest moment, but it was delicious nonetheless.

If serving it cooled down, I also recommend topping the cake with whipped cream and berries—though that's my recommendation for just about any dessert in the summertime.

Lammas (or Lughnasadh)

Lammas (*Lah*-mus) falls during a time of year ripe with the feeling of new beginnings, when summer is dwindling and children are readying themselves for their return to school. We come back to the schedules that school and work demand and slowly reintegrate our rituals of bedtimes and bath times and five-day workweeks (for those lucky enough to have summer Fridays.) The light is slowly diminishing, and we find that our days are neither quite as long, nor our mornings as early. The change of season begins to become apparent, if not in temperature then in daylight and habit.

Lammas is a quieter holiday in our Wiccan calendar. At our house, it is often the simplest of celebrations, a recognition that the turning of the year continues and the abundance of summer is waning. Lammas is the first of the three harvest festivals and is a good time to recognize how lucky we are to have everything we need so readily available. I like to spend this time of year reflecting on how far we have come as a family, how far Sam and I have come. It wasn't so long ago that we couldn't possibly dream we'd be living the life we have now, in the city we love with a happy family.

Lammas signifies an official transition state, the growth and change that can happen as we leave summer behind and prepare for the colder months. The harvest is brought in, gardens are cultivated, food is prepared and stored for the coming lean times. Today, we still go through these transitions, and while they might not be for fear of lack of food later, the run of summer into fall remains full of firsts and preparations. In our house, the beginning of the school year is inevitably the most notable of these. I once thought it would be merely a transition I needed to shepherd the children through, but I have found it also often marks a time when I realize how quickly time is passing and how big they are growing. Starting school just has a way of doing that: the first-day photos, the gathering of supplies, the ordering of uniforms. Lammas reminds me to be gentle with myself as the year turns, to be gentle with those around me as we slowly adjust to the increasing darkness and the evolution it brings with it.

Samaire's first preparations for "big kid" school were fairly intimidating. Finding a school for her here in the city had been incredibly stressful, and when we won a lottery to one of the city's best charter schools, we felt unbelievably lucky. They required uniforms, though, and it was something I was having a hard time with, on top of trying to come to terms with the fact that it was just yesterday my daughter was a tiny baby, and now suddenly she was standing before me as we waited outside the school's giant doors for her to be measured for her very first school uniform, a very important outfit.

It was pretty impersonal, of course, a big cafeteria filled with people in simple navy slacks and white shirts, smiling widely as they motioned each child and their parents over with one hand, clutching a tape measure in the other. Sam and I were wholly unprepared to answer the uniform representative's questions: How many dresses would we need? How many shirts? She was kind and offered advice and comforted us with the knowledge that we could always order more. Of course we could.

Samaire and I wandered to the big table with the sample pieces laid out while Sam and Wylie paid what we owed. Samaire scrunched her nose and made faces. There were no pinks, no purples, not even bright greens or blues. Everything was gray plaid and navy and orange. Even I had to admit it looked pretty unimpressive, piled there on a cafeteria table.

Samaire, as soon as she was able, loved to dress herself. She was regularly dressed in a combination of bright colors and sequins, and I often praised her for the unconventional, yet surprisingly successful results. She declared loudly and resoundingly exactly who she was every morning as she chose just the right shirt-and-skirt-and-variously-accessorized ensemble, something that both awed me and made my artist's heart extremely proud every time. Her closet burst with only the brightest and happiest of colors, which seemed to somehow perfectly reflect her joyful spirit.

I didn't pretend to be excited over the display in front of us, or even to think it was all exciting and pretty. Samaire would know I was faking it; she is my clone, after all. We don't fake well, and we read people like we read our many books: quickly, accurately, and deeply. So I didn't bother. I wasn't negative about it, either—just not overly enthused.

"So, kiddo, what do you think? Can you do this for me and Daddy for school?"

She paused and poked at the dress, asking where the shirts were. I picked one up and held it in front of her.

"Where's my dress again?"

I held up the dress, and she eyed it dubiously. And then she saw the backpack, the bright blue backpack with the school logo prominently embroidered on the front. I saw it, too.

"Samaire—do you see what this is?!"

She smiled. It was emblazoned across the backpack, and there again on the shirt, and again on the dress—*everywhere.*

"*Mama!* It's my *initials!*"

And yes, there they were, surrounded by a sun with rays shooting out of it: the initials of my little sunshine, SA.

Sure, they can say all they want that it stands for "Success Academy," but to us it is and always will be for Samaire Alice.

"It's not so bad," she said. "That part is pretty."

Yes, love. Indeed. "Pretty letters for a pretty girl. I think you'll look beautiful in all of it."

"Will you put pretty ribbons in my hair?"

"Every. Single. Day."

The transition was tough, but we got through, as we do with all big changes. Samaire wore her uniform and eventually thought nothing of a closet full of orange and blue. It became just another aspect of the season. We were lucky to have a school with teachers she loved and a curriculum that challenged her. She knew it. We knew it. Those orange-and-blue jumpers were a signifier not of a lack of imagination but of a plethora of blessings: a good school, wonderful friends, rising opportunity.

Lammas reminds us that there is transition this time of year, but we will reap what we sow. We must find the light as it diminishes and welcome the changes to come with open hearts. The changes themselves often point to how lucky we are, despite how uncomfortable they may seem at first. They are a chance to grow, to become better, stronger, braver.

This time of year is when we prepare for that growth, when we recognize its potential and store up what we will need in the coming months to nourish it. We look in our hearts for ways to be truly grateful for it.

This first harvest holiday is exactly that to me, a chance to be grateful. Once, Lammas was centered on the first grains brought in from the fields. It was considered bad luck to bring them in before, and so when the first grains were cut, they were ceremonially made into a loaf of bread to celebrate the previous year's harvest having been enough to sustain life until the next. This bread was shared, with the wish that the harvest would always be plentiful and those fed by it would never go unnourished.

I am lucky to live in a world where I do not have to worry if I will have enough food to feed my family through the colder months. My life is not defined by harvests succeeding or failing. Yet this turn of the year still calls for me to be grateful. I recognize how lucky we are to be in a place where I am able to nourish not only my body, through healthy food, but my mind and soul. As the year turns toward the darker months, I know our family will be able to develop and flourish, without fear of want. And for that I am deeply grateful. So, when Lammas comes around and we are busy relishing the last weeks of school-free summer and compiling lists of what we might need in the coming month as school schedules and work and after-school care collide and never coincide, I take a moment to recognize how lucky we are.

We invite friends over and sit in the garden in the dying light of the evening. I bake a loaf of bread and we share a bottle of wine and—if but for a moment—we take the time to wish, to hope, that we will always be this happy, this healthy, and this blessed.

LAMMAS BREAD

- 2 teaspoons sugar
- 2 cups lukewarm water
- 1 packet active dry yeast
- 4 cups unbleached all-purpose flour or bread flour
- 2 teaspoons kosher salt
  Butter or cooking spray for greasing the baking pan(s)
  A handful of fresh-cut herbs (sage, or a mixture of parsley, oregano, and thyme, but anything will work)

Dissolve the sugar in the water (which should be just warm, not hot) and pour the yeast over the water. The yeast should bubble up and get super foamy. This is great to have the kids do, as it's an incredibly satisfying and fun reaction to watch.

In another medium-sized bowl, mix together the flour and the salt. Once the yeast is nice and foamy, mix it up and then pour it into the flour mixture. Stir this up until the flour is no longer visible and is completely mixed into the wet ingredients. Cover the bowl with a towel and let rise in a nice warm space (again, I often warm my oven, then turn it off and let the dough rise there). Let it rise for at least an hour. It should just about double in size.

When about 45 minutes have passed, butter your baking containers. You can use an oven-safe bowl for a nice round loaf, halve the dough for use in a typical loaf pan, or even make mini-loaves in a cupcake or popover pan. I often just use my Dutch ovens and split the dough into two batches. If you're feeling particularly lazy, as I often am, go ahead and throw some parchment paper into the Dutch oven to make it easy to lift out once the bread is cooked.

Preheat the oven to 450 degrees Fahrenheit.

Punch down your dough and release it from the sides of the bowl. You will want to make sure it's not sticking anywhere to ease the process of getting it out, and make sure you've released the air built up in all of it. Now, separate it according to how you want to bake it and put it in the baking containers.

Let the dough rise again. It should rise to just above the top of whatever you're cooking it in. This, for me, takes about 30 minutes. I wouldn't do less than 20.

At this point, I like to take small pieces of dough to create designs on the top of the loaf or use a knife to carve simple symbols. It adds a bit of interest and is a reminder that this loaf is something special.

Once the dough has risen, bake for 15 minutes. Then reduce the oven temperature to 350 and bake for 20 minutes longer. I then pull my loaves out of the oven and brush melted butter over the tops of them and sprinkle them with sea salt and fresh herbs.

The herbs, always abundant this time of year, I choose for what they stand for. I use thyme for courage in facing the transitions that we will go through in the coming months. Parsley is associated with transition, and oregano is for joy.

After all, we shall reap what we sow, and bringing joyful energy to these transitions will beget joyful outcomes. Dip your bread into delicious olive oil (fruitfulness and security) and toast with a glass of wine. Wish for those around you that the nourishment and happiness they're experiencing right now may follow them always.

MABON (AUTUMN EQUINOX)

Mabon (*Mah-bahn*) falls halfway between Litha and Yule and is a day when there is an equal amount of both light and dark, the opposite of Ostara on the calendar. It is the second harvest festival, and a time to rest and reflect as well as plan and look forward, as the current year draws to its close and a new year edges toward beginning on Samhain.

Equanimity is the theme of this day, a recognition that we must always strive to keep balance in our lives. This is a conversation that happens constantly in our society, and Mabon offers a chance for us to reflect on what exactly it means in our own lives. I often struggle with feeling pulled in too many directions: mother, employee, friend, wife. I feel I'm not doing any of these roles full service, always failing at one while I focus on another. For a long time, I felt the balance of the season, the balance of the day, was about reminding me to balance my own life, to create equilibrium. The thing is, I have since realized that just as the sun wobbles on its axis, moving Mabon a day or two forward or backward every year, I, too, am allowed a little sway.

Mabon does not require that we have perfect balance in our lives but rather that we be conscious of how we are spending our time. It is a reminder that no one thing should tip our existence by happenstance, that it is only when we are acting with intention and aware of the choices we are making that we can create a balance in our hearts.

I will never be the perfect wife, mother, friend, or employee. Something will always have to give a little. However, when I am intentional, I make choices that provide me more balance than otherwise. When I make conscious choices about how I spend my time, I am better able to balance out where my energy goes. Inevitably, I will have dire deadlines and crazy workloads from time to time. I am okay with that, and if I am intentional, I put my heart into work at those times and then am able to step back and apply that same energy to being a wife and mother with the next turn of the wheel. When I am aware, when I am mindful of my choices, I am a balanced person. I am able to prioritize. I may never be able to do everything, but I can make sure I don't do one thing for so long that it takes me away from who I want to be.

Mabon is an excellent time to reflect on who that is—who I'm striving to become. It is a time for me to reflect on the choices I'm making in my life and whether or not they support those goals. It is a time for me to begin to make decisions that assure that I continue on the path I want and to dismiss the things that are getting in my way. I may never have an equal amount of energy for each thing in my life, but I have the power to control where my energy goes. I might not be able to balance my time, but I can balance my heart and who I am.

Mabon is a time of collection, a curation of what's important. It is a time to be grateful for the things we're getting right, the love and hope and support we have in our lives, and hold all of that close. Mabon is a chance to revel in what we have sown and nurtured to fruition, be that our family, our art, or our work. It is a time to gather in that which gives us strength and inspiration to put to use through the darker months.

Inspired to revel in what we have grown, every year at this time, our family makes giant pots of spaghetti sauce to have throughout winter. We use almost every vegetable we have grown in our garden, recognizing how our hard work has in turn given us this bounty. We have our last feast from our little six-by-four-foot garden plot and save the rest for a bit of brightness in the cold. The kids help gather the tomatoes and herbs. We cut the last blooms of our roses. We set a table ripe with our hard work and love.

Spaghetti Sauce

1 pint cherry tomatoes

5–8 garlic cloves, minced

Fresh oregano, basil, and parsley

4 carrots

1 Spanish onion

2 zucchini

1 red pepper

1 yellow pepper

28-ounce can of crushed tomatoes (our garden is small, y'all)

2 pounds ground sirloin, or 1 pound each sirloin and sweet & hot sausage

5 ounces garlic-and-herb cream cheese

Preheat your oven to 350 degrees Fahrenheit. Then, halve all your cherry tomatoes. Pour them onto a large baking pan and toss in olive oil and generous amounts of salt and pepper. Bake until roasted, 25 to 30 minutes, or until they are just this side of having burned edges.

While the cherry tomatoes are roasting, dice all your other herbs and vegetables. This takes a while, and I often have Sam take a shift. You might also cheat and use scissors for the herbs, unless you have an ulu knife and cutting board. (Man! We have an ulu, and it's *the best* for herbs. Thank you, Alaska.) You can use whatever herbs sound delicious to you; the ones listed above are just what we've managed to grow successfully. Regardless of what herbs you use, bunch them together and then twist them; it makes them easier to chop.

Once everything is all nicely chopped, cover the bottom of a large sauce pot in olive oil and heat to just steaming. Add in the onions and minced garlic and cook until soft over medium heat. Add in the can of tomatoes, or, if you are lucky enough to have a large garden in the suburbs somewhere, the same amount of fresh tomatoes, roughly chopped. Stir for a few minutes and then add in all your vegetables. Bring all that to a boil and then add in half of your fresh herbs.

Reduce it all to a simmer and add the cherry tomatoes. Cover and let simmer for 45 minutes. Sometimes I prefer to take the lid off for the last 20 minutes or so, to fill our apartment with delicious smells. But that's just me.

At this point, you have two options to smooth the sauce to your desired consistency. (I like it a bit chunky.) The first option is that you can use an immersion blender. Due to a tragic mishap in which I accidentally blended my finger while taking apart an immersion blender to clean on Samhain 2011, we no longer own an immersion blender. So at this point, I go with option two: let the sauce cool and then pour it in batches into my pitcher blender, pulse-blending each batch just a few times.

After this, the sauce is, in essence, done. I save a portion to use for our dinner that night, and then I freeze some of it in Ziploc bags to use in colder weather.

Before we have it for dinner, however, I like to brown some ground meat (sirloin or the mixture of sirloin with sausage) in a separate pan and drain the grease off of it well. I then stir it into the sauce along with the cream cheese until the cheese melts. Lastly, I put in the rest of the fresh herbs, and then it's ready to serve!

CHASING THE SUN

*LIVING MY FAITH IN
TIMES OF CRISIS*

I WAS RAISED REPEATEDLY HEARING TWO PHRASES: "GOD REWARDS those who follow Him" and "Good things happen to good people." So what happens when you no longer follow Him? What does it mean when bad things happen to good people? Faith and belief do not just buoy us through the everyday; they can help us face the kind of crisis that comes upon us without warning and with devastating effects.

There is a reason those events often cause a crisis of faith. Sometimes, such events can shake us to the core, so that we question everything we have ever been taught. Sometimes those events can bring up feelings and beliefs we thought we had long left behind to crash over us like a tidal wave.

It was probably one of our best summers yet. We had taken an epic weeklong vacation through Copenhagen and southern Sweden, a portion of that week having been spent with amazing friends, our chosen family. Our day in Copenhagen was one of our best ever as a family, if not the best ever. We spent that day at Tivoli Gardens, riding rides, eating tremendous amounts of ice cream and cotton candy, dressing up as pirates for lunch, and having a Michelin-starred dinner. The kids laughed and smiled more than I think I had ever seen. We watched them both find their brave, jumping on rides that would have scared them any other day and then begging to go again.

We ended the night watching our first St. John's Eve bonfire. St. John's Eve is a celebration the night before Midsummer. It celebrates St. John the Baptist's birthday and is regarded as the true shortest night of the year. It is widely believed that evil is afoot that night, and so great bonfires are built with witch effigies placed on top to ward away the wicked. It was fascinating, if a bit unnerving, to see so many figures of witches topping off giant fires. But hey, if I were an evil witch, I would have definitely flown in the other direction. So, mission accomplished.

We then walked through the winding streets of the city, witnessing several more witch-topped bonfires. We watched people gather on grassy hilltops in parks, or at the bank of the river, where the bonfires jumped and danced atop the water.

We stood for a while on a bridge, watching the fires, just the four of us. We listened to the crowds sing a Midsummer song. We played a game, trying to guess what the song's lyrics might mean. The kids, despite the late hour and their long, exciting day, watched, wide-eyed, as the small witch atop a bonfire disappeared behind the flames. I told them stories of Midsummer as the water lapped below us. We talked of fairies and witches and nights bursting with magic. We lost all track of time, the dusk lasting to midnight. We strolled through the shortest night of the year feeling lucky and loved. That night is still, and always will be, one of my most magical and treasured.

We continued the fun on a three-day layover in Iceland, and then rested for a week at home before jumping on yet another plane headed in the opposite direction to see family and spend a week in the wilds of Montana.

We continued our wonderful summer adventures at Sam's parents' cabin, filling the time with hikes and fishing and s'mores. Our last full day there, Sam and I decided we'd go for a horseback ride, just he and I. His parents and sister volunteered to help us get saddled up and then play with the kids while we went exploring. I was thrilled. Our travels had been wonderful, but they hadn't allowed for much time for just the two of us, and riding was one of my favorite activities to do at my mother- and father-in-law's ranch. Little did I know it would be my last ride for years to come.

I can't tell you with certainty what exactly happened. I know we were in an enclosed space adjacent to the barn. I know I was the first to get saddled and settled, and because I was in the back, I had to wait for Sam's horse to be saddled so Sam could jump on and we could go. I know something happened that made the other horse go wild.

My horse bucked, but I held on, trying desperately to remember everything I had been told to do in such situations. I knew my children were close by, too close by. My greatest fear every time we went to the ranch was Samaire and/or Wylie getting hurt; I didn't grow up near anything that even resembled my in-laws' ranch, and the ever-present danger of equipment and large animals there kept me constantly on guard with them, especially when we were around the horses. I knew people who had lost children to the kick of a horse, had seen a child airlifted out of a campground after a kick on my first trip to Montana. So when I realized what was happening, I immediately let go of my horse with one hand so I could turn to find my children.

"Get in the barn!" I started to yell. I almost saw them, almost found them to tell them to get so very far away, somewhere safe, before everything went sideways. I was thrown. My horse then fell toward me, landed on me, and jumped back up. The pain shot through me like an electric shock.

Then everything went quiet.

I know the horses didn't just calm immediately. I know, logically, that everything didn't just stop in that moment. I even have vague memories of watching the horses be put back in their stalls. I remember people realizing that I wasn't getting up. I have a very clear memory of my father-in-law, Fred, asking me if I *could* get up.

I remember thinking to myself of all the stories he and Sam had told me of all the times one of them was thrown, how every time, they got back up. I counted to ten in my head and willed myself to get up, but I knew it wasn't going to happen. I could see from the way my leg was turned that my knee, if not broken, was gravely damaged. When I ignored that and tried to just sit up, everything in me screamed. I remember thinking, "But I didn't hear any bones break." As much as everything hurt, I felt like I should have heard something snap, I should know for sure exactly how I had injured myself. All I knew was everything felt wrong.

I remember asking if the kids were okay. They were. Everything that mattered to me was all right.

Someone left to call an ambulance. The nearest town was far, though, so all I could do was lie on the gravel, waiting. My sister-in-law built a little lean-to so I wouldn't have to lie in the sun, and my daughter, on the teetering edge of six years old, came out to see if I was okay. She sat with me and we talked. I remember thinking I had to be okay, I had to *seem* okay, so she wouldn't be scared. I tried to make jokes. I told her to make sure to listen to her grandparents.

When the ambulance came, I remember panicking because I couldn't give her or Wylie proper hugs good-bye. I promised them I'd be home soon. I had never been away from either of them, and I needed to hear myself make that promise as much I needed them to hear it. I made them go inside before the paramedics moved me. I was determined to keep them from seeing me in pain, and I was scared that when I was moved I wouldn't be able to keep it together.

I broke the promise I had made to them and myself. I didn't come home for a long, long time, and the next time they saw me, I was definitely in pain.

After a long ride over gravel roads, a terrifying, tear-filled temporary stay in the tiny local hospital, and an emergency life flight to a bigger hospital, we discovered I had pretty much shattered the bones directly below my left knee and broken my pelvis straight through. There were other, smaller injuries I'd discover over the coming year, but those were the real winners.

I was in the ICU, then surgery, then recovery, and then, at last, on the rehabilitation floor. This was where I was going to learn to walk again. I was on a constant rotation of painkillers and blood draws. Every morning I spent a couple hours in physical therapy, and then I spent the evenings exercising as best I could. I asked the nurses to bring me arm weights. I wanted to feel strong, I wanted to try to *be* strong, somehow, on any level.

It was draining and frightening, but I was determined. I wasn't going to let pain stop me from holding my kids again, from walking with them again. No pain would keep me from dancing with my husband again. We were going to conquer more mountains together—we had more of the world to hike through. I couldn't give up. I concentrated on one moment at a time, one small task every day.

I was surviving. It was all I could do.

Physically, I was soon making small improvements. Emotionally? Mentally? Those were up for debate. And then, after a couple weeks, Sam had to go back home, to do his job and try to find us a place to live—our fifth-floor walk-up was not going to be an option any time soon.

He and the kids had been in to see me every day. It was the first time I had been away from them, and Sam knew how important it was for me to see them, how very much I needed them. I needed him, too. When he said good-bye and walked out the door, I felt like he had taken every ounce of my strength with him. The black hole I had been standing on the edge of rose up and swallowed me whole.

No spell or grounding words found me. I had lost the ability to stand and feel the weight of centuries of earth beneath my feet. I couldn't see the stars or the moon out my window. I felt lost and alone. I was drifting. Any notion of finding my spiritual center was lost in the midst of just trying to get through the next hour, the next minute.

I felt as if I couldn't breathe.

I lay there on the bed for ages and stared at the ceiling. I counted my breaths and tried desperately to summon the courage I knew was inside me somewhere. I tried to imagine a mustard seed inside my heart, imagined how it could grow mighty roots—how it could reach the sky. Still I came up empty. I blinked back tears as the anger started to well up and I tried to quell it. Who was there to be mad at? Should I rage against the injustice of it all? Sometimes I felt like it would make all the difference if I could just yell *at* someone—if I could *blame* them, hurl hurtful words and hateful speech, just get it all out *at* someone, or something.

I needed a God. In that moment, I wanted there to be one omniscient being who had planned my life for me, if only so I could be angry with Him. Shaking my fist up at the universe had very little effect on my mood. It felt too vague, too unfinished . . . too unreal.

I felt like I was being punished. To this girl, who grew up hearing over and over again, "God rewards those who follow Him," and, "Good things happen to good people," this felt like doing penance. So what if you didn't follow Him? Is this what happened? What did this make me, that something so awful could happen to me? I was spiraling, and the spiritual path that I had nurtured and grown on as I built my place and identity in this world, as I honored my own divine power, fled—while all the old beliefs I'd left behind reared up and frightened the living hell out of me. I felt alone and scared. I felt powerless.

As I sat in that place of fear, I received both a text and an email (when I didn't respond to the text right away) from a longtime family friend. *I can't help but think that perhaps God is trying to tell you something about how you live your life.*

I sat and stared at the messages. My phone, which had previously been a lifeline to the world I had been forced to leave behind, now felt heavy and cumbersome. I quickly hit delete and tried to stanch the tears before they started to flow in earnest.

I had no way to respond. No honest way, at least.

Those words were worse than a blatant curse, worse in many ways than the accident itself. Once I'd read them, no matter what I did, where I turned, they would be there. After all, they'd been said by someone who knows me, who loves me—and who believed, at the lowest point of my life, that *I had deserved for this to happen.* This thought began to haunt me in my worst moments.

Over the coming weeks, however, my shock and sadness gave way to anger. It burned the tears away and helped me push aside a small part of the guilt I had already been carrying. Because of course, *of course* I felt guilty. My children were without their mother for the first time in their lives and far away from home. My husband was scrambling to work and find us a new home, all while being separated from his children, too. I was costing us tens of thousands of dollars. Could I have done something differently? Should I have known somehow not to ride that day? Were there signs or moments that I should have known were trying to tell me something? What had I done to deserve this?

I kept coming back to those stupid words, that meaningless phrase, *Everything happens for a reason*. That text and email merely legitimized a fear that was already pulling me under—that I deserved this punishment for some reason, that I had done something wrong. Sliding down that slope offered a chance to lay blame, and I desperately wanted someone to blame. Unfortunately, the fault just always came back to me. There was no one else.

But just when I thought the divine power in me had left, when I was too weak to stand, that small seed I hadn't been able to nurture before took root. I felt it in my heart, at my very core. I started to feel the solidity below me and the promise above me again. I started to get pieces of myself back.

And then I got angry again. This was not my fault.

People tell you that everything happens for a reason, but it is for their own good that they say it. Don't be fooled by the thin veneer of compassion the phrase is supposed to carry. Like a wolf in sheep's clothing, it is dressed as kindness when it is merely selfishness. That phrase is not for the listener but the speaker: no one wants to believe something awful could happen to them or those they love. They want to believe if they play by the rules, whatever the rules are, they will be rewarded. They will be kept safe. They want to believe some higher power is watching them live their good life and so they cannot—will not—be tried. I cannot fault that. It's not mine to say if they are right or wrong. However, I can with time learn to forgive it. I have, in fact. My relationship with the sender of that email continues despite my having never replied—as intact as it was before I read my messages that day. Our families gather together every year. Forgiving, though, does not mean accepting. That way of thinking is a path I diverged from long ago.

I, however, am a witch, and I am responsible for my own life. And sometimes life is messy and unfair and chaotic. Sometimes bad things happen to good people for no reason whatsoever. That is a frightening fact to stare down. It is also empowering. I cannot control the universe—but I can take control of my circumstances and my reaction to them.

I understood that this was not my fault, and "God" wasn't talking to me. No one was trying to tell me I had some lesson that needed learning that couldn't be taught any other way. (Can you imagine?!) I did not lose my ability to live without pain, my ability to walk; I was not forced apart from my children and husband so that I could come to heel to a god I did not believe in. I was in an accident—an unfortunate, horrible accident. And I would see the other side. I would walk again, without a cane. I would dance with my husband when we were joyful and I would carry my children when they were weary. I would find my way back, maybe not to exactly who I had been, but to myself all the same.

I would do so not because I was blessed or because it was part of a greater plan but because I would fight like hell to get there. I have the same power within me that turns the stars and created this world.

So I fought. I wavered and I stumbled, but I fought. When the pain was too much, I closed my eyes and tried to remember the feeling of that small seed growing bigger. I imagined its roots strengthening my legs, its trunk protecting my heart. I moved forward, with a determination that faltered from time to time but did not give up.

The moon travels with me through the night. I am a witch, and I have divine power at my center. I may lose sight of that from time to time, but in my heart it is who I am, and when I fall, it helps me find the strength I need to rise again.

Of course, I want to tell you that finding a spiritual path you believe in solves all your troubles—gives you unending peace, gives you bottomless reserves of hope—but I can't. I can't tell you that this path, or any path you may choose, will wipe away all the sorrow or the fear. It only gives us a light to lead the way out—or, more often than not, to merely shine in the darkness, to remind us that someday it will be the darkness that will be the small dot in the overwhelming sky. Being a witch doesn't save me from suffering or anger or sadness or defeat. It's apparent that I can't wave a wand or weave a spell that will keep my loved ones and me safe. The world spins on, and us with it, sometimes without rhyme or reason. We do our best.

That doesn't mean this incident doesn't still haunt me, years later. I'm still fighting.

I'd been back at work for a few months when I realized the fight still wasn't entirely behind me. It was one o'clock and there, on a bench where I sat with my Kindle and a turkey sandwich, the cacophony of the city was almost enough to make it truly impossible to comprehend the words in front of me. Of course, they had gone flat anyhow. A wave of undeniable fear had been building behind me for over a day now. I felt it tug at my feet, felt the world pull back slowly, slowly. I kept my head down and concentrated on positive moments: Samaire's hand in mine; a congratulatory email from my physical therapist; a kind smile on the train; Wylie's sloppy, sweet kisses goodnight; Sam's arm around my waist, holding me up in all the ways that matter most.

And still, behind me, the world continued to slowly pull away. The dread rose up from the pit in my stomach and settled in my heart. And now here, over my bland turkey sandwich, in this oh-so-public place, I wanted to curl up on the ground, my hands covering my head, as I waited for the blow. I felt the absence of breath, the overflow of tears, the sheer certainty that something wicked this way comes.

But it doesn't. It didn't. I felt wrecked nonetheless. I felt I could cry for hours unabated and still have a well to draw on. I packed up my things quickly, begged my body and mind not to betray me. Begged them to just last until I could get somewhere, anywhere private. I gulped giant breaths of air and determinedly pushed back the tears. I fought my demons. I fought myself.

Everything was fine. Everything was fine. Everything was fine. Everything was fine. Everything was fine.

Everywhere I looked, there was the potential for disaster. I took deep breaths and concentrated on the good. I thought about how Samaire and Wylie were safe; I fought the overwhelming need to call their school to be sure. I planned what I would fix them for dinner, what questions I'd bombard them with when I saw them next. I imagined them and Sam and I all crowded onto our couch, watching a show that inevitably only half of us were ever interested in—but all avidly watching nonetheless. I thought about my next painting, my next project.

I took really deep breaths. I thought about my yoga instructor and the way she had taught me to breathe that week. I practiced it once, twice, three times.

I held my bag tighter to quell the shaking of my hands and headed back to where I needed to be in that moment: where in-depth discussions revolved around fonts and palettes and people sniped about emails. I pulled open the door and let a smile spread across my face as far as I could manage. I plunged back into what felt like a whole other world. I sat in the sun on a small couch and typed out a brief.

My heartbeat slowed, and the world slowly tipped toward normality.

Talking about it all no longer makes me cry. I may never be rid of my fears; perhaps none of us will. But I can stop letting them conquer me. These days, I can tell you about my accident in sordid detail and do so without feeling like a wound freshly opened. I will still pause in places—I will still catch my breath a bit when I think about the fact that Samaire or Wylie could have been kicked, could have been the ones hurt. But I can smile now through the part where (if I feel you are okay with knowing) I tell you that it could have been much worse: I could have not made it to the other side of this. It was just inches and luck and hair's breadths that kept my heart beating, kept my soul tied to those I love most for a while longer.

But I got those inches. I got a chance at sharing this adventure with my loved ones for a while longer. I survived it through the power I had within myself, and when I was weak, my loved ones lent me theirs. None of it was an act of a benevolent or rageful god. I was just in the wrong place at the wrong time, and through sheer force of heart, I survived it. On my own divine power, I survive it still.

That feels really good to say.

OH OH OH
IT'S MAGIC

A F T E R W O R D

So NOW YOU KNOW THE WITCH'S SECRET: MAGIC IS NO MORE OR LESS than recognizing and acknowledging the wonder in this world. It is being able to harness that wonder and create some magic ourselves. It is not just being in tune with the energy around us but trusting the energy inside of us. It is listening to our intuition, to the whispering of our hearts and how they speak to the world—and to how the world speaks to us and what it has to say.

Magic is doing what needs to be done. It's being able to relieve a bit of the pain of someone who is hurting, to carry a bit of their burden when we have the strength to spare, and sometimes even when we do not. It is noticing someone who feels lost and making him or her truly feel seen; it is holding the hand of someone who might need to borrow some courage or baking bread for someone who needs to feel loved.

Being a witch isn't conjuring; it's connecting. It's not about a third eye or second sight—rather, it is taking the time to really see what is around you and choosing to make it better, brighter, kinder. It is not just invoking, it is *involving*, deciding to truly be a force in the world we inhabit—to be an active part of the wondrous cycle that moves us all.

Wicca is not about spells and concoctions to bring love or luck or money. It's about being the wealth and love that is needed for yourself and those around you. It's about making your own luck by seizing opportunities and recognizing moments of synchronicity. It is so much more than the dull, expected definition of what is magical—it is empowering yourself to join in with a greater force to become truly mystical. Not just for the big things, but for all the little things in between.

Sure, Wicca is my religion, and being a witch is who I am deep in my heart, but I honestly believe there's a little witch in all of us. Within each of us resides the potential and promise of magic. We can all bring light into the world if we choose to; we all can reach out into a dark abyss and find hope and wonder. Each of us knows what it's like to whisper a small hope into the moonlight, setting it on a course we cannot control, keeping our heart open for it to come echoing back to us.

So there you have it. We have created magic just now, you and I: the witch finally made it all the way to the end of the story in one piece! How often does that happen?! So cheers to us. Cheers to you. Cheers to our amazing, connected, beautiful world and all the divine power lying in wait for us to create an even more magical and meaningful one.

So mote it be—a phrase repeated endlessly in Wiccan texts of spells. I say it, I put my heart behind it, I let it happen with greatest of intention.

So mote it be.

NOTES

I grew up with some talented musicians who taught me early on the power a string of just the right words set to just the right notes can have. Nathan Tysen and Ryan McCall created magic in our small coffee shop in Salina, Kansas, when we were all just teenagers and fueled in me a lifelong true love of that very sort of enchantment. A certain song or lyric can take me straight back to a specific moment in time like very little else can. It also buoys me in times of struggle, and has the power absolutely to make me feel invincible. As I look back on the years I have lived so far, I can immediately list the songs that have accompanied me, that have followed me . . . that have inspired me. So naturally, as I wrote this book and drew these pictures, music escorted me along the way. I have included some small references that felt true and right here in my chapter titles. A list follows to give the credit due to the songs' creators. If you want the audio playlist, a link to it can be accessed by visiting, www.apollopublishers.com.

Everyone Deserves the Chance to Fly
    "Defying Gravity" / *Kristin Chenoweth and Idina Menzel*

That's Me in the Corner
    "Losing My Religion" / *R.E.M.*

A Little Faith and a Lot of Heart
    "Stars" / *The Weepies*

A Restless Spirit on an Endless Flight
    "Witchy Woman" / *Eagles*

That's the Power Makes the World Go Round
    "The Power of Love" / *Huey Lewis and the News*

I Light a Candle Then I Call Your Name
    "Georgia O" / *The Nields*

I Put a Spell on You
    "I Put a Spell on You" / *Jeff Beck and Joss Stone*

Big Wheel Keep on Turnin'
    "Proud Mary" / *Tina Turner*

These Are the Days of Miracle and Wonder
    "Boy in the Bubble" / *Paul Simon*

And We'll Dance by the Light of the Moon
    "Buffalo Gals" / *Bruce Springsteen*

Chasing the Sun
    "Chasing the Sun" / *Sara Bareilles*

Oh Oh Oh It's Magic
    "Magic" / *Pilot*

ACKNOWLEDGMENTS

Writing my gratitude to the people who brought me here, to the last page of my book, seems an impossible task. Words on a page will never be enough to express how deeply I am indebted to those I'm about to list, and I shall inevitably not thank all I should. I am doomed to mess this up. And yet, true to form, I'm blindly plowing forward nonetheless.

Thank you, Amy Choi of MashupAmericans.com, for asking to hear my story that first time, and finding it worthy to share. Thank you, Julia Abramoff and Apollo Publishers, for seeing potential in that first interview and taking a chance on a girl who before had only dreamt of writing a book.

Molly Lindley Pisani, you held my hand through this entire process in a way there will never be enough thanks for, while taking the utmost care to make sure I was able to convey my story in the best way possible. Your patience and attention is something I will forever hold dear.

Cordelia, thank you for saying you'd read this when it was just a kernel of an idea. Cathe, May, and Leslie, thank you for helping me work through those ideas and being right there with me day after day reading snippets and celebrating every small victory. Sometimes a girl just needs a cheer squad; I could not ask for better.

Thank you to Alberto Mier, whose friendship has been one of my most treasured from that first day in the school store, and whose artistic advice and constant inspiration contributed in no small way to the art in this book.

Kase and Mary, you came through with endless advice, guidance, and support in that way only family can. I'm so glad you're mine.

I honestly don't know what I would do without you, Molly Connor.

You somehow know how to reach across the miles and hold my hand when I need it most. Thank you for being such an incredibly kick-ass friend, first reader, and first-grade compatriot.

Hitha, you are golden for reminding me when I am exhausted and convinced I have somehow been miscast that I deserve a seat at the table—in every part of my life. New York is what it is to me in large part due to your unwavering friendship.

And last but not least, Sam. This book is as much yours as it is mine. Thank you for giving me the time and space I needed to get it written, for sponsoring innumerable weekends at Starbucks, for reminding me on those late nights this would be worth it, and for giving me the best reason of all to break open my heart and share it with the world, our own small acts of magic: Samaire Alice and Wylie William. Samuel Henry, you make me feel like a true goddess every day. Thank you for working with me to build a life more wonderful than any I could ever conjure.